SEP 2021

The
INVISIBLE
DEAL

Why Mobile Homes Are The Perfect Investment
and How to Flip, Wholesale, and Rent Them

MATEO NICOLAS

Mount Laurel Library
100 Walt Whitman Avenue
Mount Laurel, NJ 08054-9539
856-234-7319
www.mountlaurellibrary.org

Copyright © 2020 by Mateo Nicolas. All rights reserved.

The content contained within this book may not be reproduced, duplicated or transmitted without direct written permission from the author or the publisher.

Under no circumstances will any blame or legal responsibility be held against the publisher, or author, for any damages, reparation, or monetary loss due to the information contained within this book, either directly or indirectly.

Legal Notice:
This book is copyright protected. It is only for personal use. You cannot amend, distribute, sell, use, quote or paraphrase any part, or the content within this book, without the consent of the author or publisher.

Disclaimer Notice:
Please note the information contained within this document is for educational and entertainment purposes only. All effort has been executed to present accurate, up-to-date, reliable, complete information. No warranties of any kind are declared or implied. Readers acknowledge that the author is not engaged in the rendering of legal, financial, medical or professional advice. The content within this book has been derived from various sources. Please consult a licensed professional before attempting any techniques outlined in this book.

By reading this document, the reader agrees that under no circumstances is the author responsible for any losses, direct or indirect, that are incurred as a result of the use of the information contained within this document, including, but not limited to, errors, omissions, or inaccuracies.

Printed in the United States of America.

Cover Design by 100Covers.com
Interior Design by FormattedBooks.com

CONTENTS

PART 1. THE NUTS AND BOLTS OF MOBILE HOME INVESTING

Chapter 1: The Basics: Everything you need to know about Mobile Home Investing 15

Chapter 2: The Three Most Profitable Ways To Invest In Mobile Homes 35

PART 2. THE ULTIMATE STEP-BY-STEP GUIDE TO FINDING YOUR FIRST INVESTMENT THIS MONTH

Chapter 3: Step 1: How To Find A Profitable Deal........63

Chapter 4: Step 2: The Experienced Investor's Secret to Due Diligence and Walkthroughs ...89

Chapter 5: Step 3: How to Determine What The Mobile Home Is Worth And Negotiate A Discount 111

Chapter 6: Step 4: Profit!...135

PART 1

THE NUTS AND BOLTS OF MOBILE HOME INVESTING

ADDRESSING THE MYTHS (READ THIS IF YOU'RE A SKEPTIC OR A DOUBTER)

Myth: Mobile homes are depreciating assets so you can't make any money on them

Many new investors make the mistake of believing that you can only make money when your asset appreciates. Sure, if you're investing in conventional residential real estate, the appreciation is what you're looking for because you usually won't have a fantastic cashflow while you're paying your loan off.

However, mobile homes are a different game completely. As depreciating assets, you can purchase gently used mobile homes for a fraction of the price of a new one (which are also much cheaper than their counterparts in the residential real estate world). Investors do not invest in mobile homes because they are hoping that it will appreciate in 30 years… they invest for the near immediate cash flow.

Myth: Investing in mobile homes has no advantage over more conventional investments

Advantage #1: You can find absolute GEMS for almost nothing. Seriously, many mobile home investors regularly find flips for as little as $3000 that just need $2000 worth of work to turn them into a $25,000 sale! Can you imagine making $20,000 from a $5,000 investment? Those are insane numbers!

Advantage #2: Since they are seen as depreciating assets, most other investors will stay away from them. Many new investors believe that appreciation is key when you invest in real estate. While appreciation is nice, we do have a saying in this business: "Never count on appreciation". You literally don't know what will happen. Will your city turn into San Francisco or will it turn into Memphis? If it's San Fran, you're a millionaire! If it's Memphis, you just turned $60,000 into $20,000. Since other investors stay away from mobile homes, it means the market is wide open for you. It's much more open than the residential space, which is oversaturated by investors who want to copy HGTV.

Advantage #3: Mobile homes bring nearly IMMEDIATE cash flow. For instance, let's say you buy a gently used mobile home for $10,000. More than likely, that mobile home will generate enough rent to pay itself off within two years. Now you have 30 years of pure cashflow with no mortgage. Compare that to the normal 15- or 30-year mortgage, and you can see why I love mobile homes so much. Immediate cash flow is king, especially when you are first starting out and need the money to buy more investments.

Advantage #4: Investing in mobile homes is much less risky than investing in stick-built homes (aka normal residential real estate). Since mobile homes are cheaper, you risk less when you buy them. Mobile homes also have certain qualities that make finding problems on an initial walkthrough much easier. For example, the piping and foundation are completely exposed under the house, so you can spot many problems on the first look. We will go over how to find out if a prospective mobile home is a deal or a dud later, but it takes much less experience to find problems. You don't need me to tell you that this massively decreases the risk of purchasing a dud, even if you're a new investor!

Advantage #5: You can get some of them for free! Since mobile homes are a depreciating asset, many families choose to upgrade every 20 or 30 years. When a family upgrades, they have to get rid of their old mobile home. Oftentimes, they will solve this problem by selling it to the same dealer that is selling them their new mobile home. The dealer doesn't want these old homes because they take a lot of effort to sell and are generally not profitable to store, upkeep and showcase. In fact, most dealers find it cheaper to pay to transport them to a dump than showcase them! These mobile homes are usually perfectly fine and really don't belong in a dump.

That's where you, a savvy investor, come in. More on this later!

Myth: No one will want to rent or buy a mobile home!

Believe it or not, mobile homes are one of the fastest growing housing options out there[1]. Millennials who want to purchase their first home have been forced into finding a cheaper alternative to stick-built homes. Sure, some of them get around this by purchasing a house and renting out the rooms but, a growing number of them purchase mobile homes because they like having their own space for an affordable price.

The stigma around mobile homes is quickly changing as more and more people realize that buying a mobile home is like having a 50% off coupon for a house. This translates well into rentals. While you might not be able to rent out a mobile home for the same price as a residential stick-built home, you can still turn a great ROI and find **excellent** renters. In fact, I try to find renters that have a credit score of 680 and above with zero red flags on their background check. If that isn't at least close to what you look for when you rent out your stick-built homes, then you're way too picky.

As for the cash flow, I personally only invest in a mobile home if it gives me $500 in revenue each month. That means I have $500 in pure profit even after lot rent, mortgage, and any other expenses. Imagine if you could buy 2 mobile homes like that each year. That would be an extra $1000/month or $12,000 your very first year.

Myth: I can't possibly invest because I'm too young!

Getting started young is actually an advantage.

First, you have a lot more energy than people who start investing later in life.

Second, you feel like you can take on the world. When you're young, you're bold. As you get older, this feeling fades.

Third, you can make mistakes and quickly recover from them because you don't have a lot to lose. As you get older you become more and more afraid of making mistakes because the risks are a lot higher. But when you're 18, you own almost nothing and can probably move back home or crash on a friend's couch if things really go south.

If you're a young person who is on the fence about investing because you don't know what you're doing, then you'll be happy to learn that no new investor really knows what they are doing. Getting older does not give you all the information you need to invest in real estate perfectly. The only thing that will give you all the knowledge you need is actually getting your hands dirty and trying to invest. So, the sooner you start, the sooner you'll know what you're doing.

So if you're young but you have a few thousand dollars saved up, a car, and the will to create financial independence, then keep reading!

Myth: I can't invest in real estate because I'm too old!

Just like young investors, older investors have some advantages as well.

You usually have more experience negotiating and have more money saved up.

You also fit the general investing demographic. Most people don't become interested in investing until they realize that they would like to retire soon but haven't saved enough money.

That said, investing in mobile homes is the perfect investment for those getting started late because you won't have to wait 30 years before you turn a serious profit. In fact, you can start making bank in less than a year! Later on in this book, I show you how you can own 5 mobile homes within 2 years. If you're looking to retire soon (or have a major expense like your child's college tuition!) then you will love that section.

Myth: I can't invest in real estate - it's too expensive!

This is 100% true if you are trying to follow the HGTV trend and purchase stick-built homes. There are some gurus out there that insist that you can find deals for $20,000-$50,000. Those deals exist but they are becoming less and less common and usually require a lot of work. In contrast, if you're spending $20,000 on a mobile home, you're most likely purchasing a very well kept single-wide that is already ready to rent.

Truth: Mobile homes are *invisible deals*

Mobile homes are a great investment for those of us who are looking for a real estate market that is cheap, unsaturated, and profitable.

If that's all true, why are they so overlooked?

The answer to that is simple: most investors believe all the myths I just debunked! They believe you'll only get flight-risk renters, you won't make any money, and no one wants to buy or rent them anyway. For these mainstream investors, mobile homes *may as well be invisible*.

Fortunately for you, they don't know what they're missing.

As a thank you, here's $100 worth of tools that will make your mobile home investments easier for free!

Free Bonus #1 Mobile Home Profit Analyzer ($59 value)

We all know the saying: good investors have a calculator, great investors have a spreadsheet. Well, ok maybe I just made that up. Either way, a good profit analyzer spreadsheet is worth its weight in gold! As a thank you, I'd like to give you the very same spreadsheet I use for analyzing deals. It includes a rehab and a rental calculator. This spreadsheet is instrumental in helping me understand if I have a deal or a dud within 10 minutes!

Free Bonus #2 Mobile Home Investment Checklist ($29 value)

Finding a mobile home is only half the battle; you also need to know what problems to look for! This checklist is an organized list of all the problems a mobile home can have that you can use when you walk through a mobile home. It's also a very useful tool when you are trying to negotiate a discount because it's a very easy way for the seller to realize there is a lot wrong with their property and goes a long way towards convincing them you deserve a discount.

Free Bonus #3 Mobile Home FSBO Script ($12 value)

Most new investors are excited to get started... but deathly afraid of their first phone call. I want to blow that fear away with my Mobile Home FSBO owner script. This script will make you sound like a pro from your very first deal. This script has all of the questions you need to ask any seller. That way, you always know what to ask when a new lead gives you a call!

All of this is 100% free when you subscribe to our free mobile home investing newsletter.

To get your free bonuses go to www.MateosMobiles. com/mobiles

INTRODUCTION

> "Landlords grow rich in their sleep
> without working, risking or economizing."
> —John Stuart Mill

Like most investors, I used to think mobile homes were trashy assets. What's the point of buying a depreciating asset anyway? Wouldn't it just be worthless in 30 years? I stuck to "safe" real estate - residential, land and notes.

One afternoon, I stopped at my company's security desk to ask if I had received any mail. I was met by an unfamiliar face - a new security guard that my company had hired just recently named Mark. He was my age (24), had two full sleeve tattoos and was very friendly.

We were friends for almost a year before I invited him over for some drinks at my place. I was shocked to learn that he drove around in a brand new corvette! How could a security guard afford a car like that? And more importantly, why didn't I have one?

That's when I found out he had over $10,000 coming in each month in pure profit from a small mobile home park that he was building and running on top of his normal 9-5 job. Why would he be working for $15/hour if he had a full $120,000 coming in from a mobile home park?

Like most people interested in investing, Mark was willing to work hard now so he didn't have to work at all later! So, he used the money from his day job to live, and the profit from his mobile home park to invest!

He had purchased 10 acres of land out in the sticks for a little over $2000 per acre. It was a sizable purchase for him at the time because he didn't have much in savings. After all, he was just a security guard (yep! even then). In fact, he took out a personal loan to buy the land and threw a janky old trailer on it that was basically on its way to the dump before he saved it.

He scrimped and saved until he had just enough for another one. And another one. And another - until he had six mobile homes on his 10-acre lot. And you better believe he will have 10 by the end of 2022.

As someone who had quite a bit of knowledge about investing in land, I decided that buying mobile homes was the way to go. Mark showed me the light. And since then, I've discovered a multitude of ways that you can invest in mobile homes. I'll share the three most profitable with you in this book.

Who am I and why should you listen to me?

I'm Mateo. I've bought online courses worth tens of thousands of dollars and found that all of them were... let's just say... lacking. I've met hundreds of new investors who paid their $50,000 entry fee into a guru's inner fold, only to watch them quit investing. So, I set out to condense lots of insider knowledge into this book for a fraction of the cost. My goal is to help new investors see that there are a hundred ways to skin a cat, so to speak, and you don't just have to invest in residential real estate! Do not fall victim to believing you have to invest like you're on HGTV. There is more out there than what is popular!

Why Mobile Homes?

There are really only two reasons anyone would try to invest in real estate:

1. They want to retire early.
2. They want to create a reliable stream of income for their family.

Real estate investing has been one of the most reliable ways of building wealth in America. This makes sense when you think about it. Real estate is, well, real - it's tangible. You can point to it and proudly say "That's mine." There are very few other investment methods that give you that kind of advantage. If you invest in stocks, what can you point to? A few pieces of paper? Some electronic symbols that go up and down and that mean nothing to you? Nothing compares to the solidity of a real estate investment.

Mobile home investing is not often talked about among investors. Why? Because investors are OBSESSED with appreciating assets. Many won't even consider purchasing a property unless they believe it's going to almost double in value by the time they've finished paying the mortgage. Well, I for one am here to say that appreciation in 30 years doesn't really matter if you want to become financially independent *right now*. If you want to be financially independent and quit your job in a few years, wouldn't you care more about immediate cash flow?

Mobile homes are a great investment option. They're inexpensive to purchase and they produce great cash flow each month. Since the cashflow is so high, you can use it to quickly pay the one you purchased off and save up a down payment for another. If you're an excellent negotiator, you might even end up putting $0 down.

Despite being a great way to build wealth, some people lose money investing in mobile homes. Why is this? Put simply, it's because they rush in without taking the time to educate themselves. By reading this book and deciding to study first, you've taken a great step and dramatically reduced your probability of losing money.

I'm going to show you how you can safely navigate the world of mobile home investing and how you can avoid the most common pitfalls that beginner investors fall into. By the end of this book, you should know exactly what you need to do to move forward. And you should feel confident enough to actually do it.

1

THE BASICS: EVERYTHING YOU NEED TO KNOW ABOUT MOBILE HOME INVESTING

Before investing in anything, I like to know everything about it. You might think that mobile homes are pretty simple, but you're wrong. They're a world in and of themselves.

What is a mobile home?

There are more than 10 major mobile home manufacturers and all of them have different quality and style. If you go on Champion's website (the biggest mobile home manufacturer in the world), you will see that a lot of the mobile homes look quite stylish and updated on the inside.

Mobile homes are generally manufactured in a factory and then transported to their final destination. You may have heard the term "pre-fabricated". They're designed to a high standard and are manufactured to federal guidelines, which were significantly updated in 1985. It's important you remember that year, because while I advise you to purchase gently-used mobile homes, you should never purchase a mobile home that is older than 1985 because it will almost literally fall apart if you try to move it.

Being built in a factory is a huge advantage that mobile homes have over stick-built houses, because the temperatures and climate are controlled. The workers also have a much better experience building the home because they are in an air-conditioned factory instead of out in the heat, snow, or rain. Compare that to your average outdoor residential neighborhood construction project. Any new home has its bare wood and construction workers exposed to the elements for at least a few weeks.

Once the home is manufactured, it will be transported to your location and installed on site. Think of it as ordering a custom made product from a factory. You can tell them exactly what you want and have it delivered to you. Best of all, if you decide to move somewhere else, you can take your home with you! How cool is that? Mobile homes are perhaps better described by calling them "prefabricated living units" but that's a mouthful, so I'm going to stick to mobile homes instead.

What do Mobile Homes Look Like?

The development of factories that could prefabricate and transport homes was a massive blessing to prospective homeowners across America. Prefabbed homes allow you to invest in real estate while avoiding the massive costs that typically come with it. Mobile homes are referred to by many names. Some of these are house trailers, trailer homes, trailers, static caravans, or residential caravans.

Notice that the words trailers and caravans pop up quite a lot. This is why the image of a trailer on wheels is the one most associated with mobile homes. However, the typical mobile home has an entrance, windows, and can have up to five bedrooms, along with all the bells and whistles you would expect in a conventional home. It can even have a front patio and steps leading up to the front door.

With that being said, mobile homes are usually single stories, though there are some modular homes than can be more. However, most of the mobile homes you will see in parks will be either a single-wide or a double-wide home. The double-wide homes are excellent houses for investing because they have more interior space.

The average mobile home is smaller than the average suburban property simply because they need to be transported as a whole on a truck. However, these homes are spacious enough for the average family of 4.5 to live comfortably. In fact, I have been in many double-wide homes that have 5 bedrooms, 3 bathrooms, a kitchen and a living room!

Modular Homes

While looking through mobile home manufacturer websites (or even just driving through parks) you will see a variety of different types of housing. Modular homes are one such type. In general, modular homes are manufactured as separate units and assembled onsite. They are also almost always permanently attached to land and are considered real estate for tax purposes. Since these modular homes are considered real estate, banks will more easily finance them.

Another bonus to modular homes is that they look a lot more like conventional real estate. They have multiple stories, don't have to be shaped like a rectangle, and can have more complex designs. It can be very easy to think that these homes are conventional real estate! In fact, I had a few friends who got into the final stages of purchasing one before their inspector told them that it was a modular home, which wouldn't have been bad if the sellers didn't want $350,000 for it!

Manufactured Homes

Manufactured homes are more of what you think of when you think of mobile homes in parks. These homes are more of what you will be investing in when you start investing in mobile homes, because 99% of mobile home parks have these manufactured homes in them as opposed to the other types - Park Model RVs and Modular Homes. This type of home is most commonly seen as a single-wide or a double-wide, however they can be wider (the rare multi-wide home!) They normally have a chassis, axle, and wheels so that they can be easily moved from location to location.

If your investment is this type of mobile home, you must permanently affix it and apply for real estate status. This changes your tax implications but you will find that since mobile homes are worth less than conventional real estate, the taxes you pay are still comparatively minute.

Park Model RV

These mobile homes are extremely small and often look like a rectangle with wheels on the bottom. If you are investing in a vacation home or an RV park, then this is your go-to! These homes are no larger than 400 square feet and are always considered recreational vehicles. This means they can never reach real estate status, they are always considered personal property.

Park Model Homes are popular for use as a cottage, a cabin, a vacation home, or a retirement home. They are extremely affordable and designed with efficiency and style in mind, containing as many amenities as possible while also maintaining a stylish living space. They are connected to utilities just like any of the other mobile home varieties and can reside in any climate.

This type of Mobile Home is best for investing in vacation rentals. If you wanted to buy some land on a lake and place some mobile homes around it for a short term rental, then this is the perfect investment. Since these are so small, they normally just have a kitchen, a small living area, one bed, and one bathroom. They might also be great if you are investing in a college town or a tech hub as there are a lot of young, single people in these areas that would love to have their own space but don't want to live in an apartment complex.

Travel Trailers

Travel Trailers are another type of mobile home, though you might have to get creative if you want to invest in them. They are typically used as temporary living arrangements or vacation homes. People usually hitch them to the back of their vehicles and transport them wherever they're going. (Sometimes, they even ARE a vehicle!)

I knew an investor who bought a beautiful acre lot on a lake near me. He didn't want to subdivide it and it was kind of out in the middle of nowhere, so his options were a bit limited. He knew he probably wouldn't get a lot of cashflow if he built a house, so he had to get creative. What he decided to do was purchase two used travel trailers and place them on the land. He hired a sewage company to come once a week to take care of the waste water and charged the residents with the extra cost. That's some creative investing, there!

Durability

People often wonder whether mobile homes are durable. My answer to this question is that they last as long as the average home in suburbia lasts. Assuming normal weather conditions and regular maintenance, you can expect a mobile home to last between 30-55 years[6].

I've walked through some 20-year-old residential homes that were an absolute doozy. I've also walked through some 20-year-old mobile homes that looked as pristine as the day the owners bought them. Like any real estate, the state of the home depends on the care the previous owner gave it.

Mobile homes are built to exacting federal guidelines. The process usually begins by manufacturing the steel frame upon which the house rests. This is created by welding steel beams together to create a sturdy skeleton. On top of this, insulation layers are added to make the structure energy efficient. The next step of the process sees floors and walls added. Finally, the roof is placed on top of the structure.

The final step is an inspection for safety according to federal guidelines. Once the structure passes inspection, it's transported to your site. The manufacturer will unload your home and set it into its foundations to make sure it's well rooted to the land. Throughout that process, you can request changes and customization to the interior. The manufacturer will typically assume all responsibility for damage during transportation and other issues that might arise shortly after. If the mobile home is used, the transportation company assumes all risks during transport.

If you're planning on buying a brand new home and moving it to a location, the task of moving your mobile home is coordinated between the manufacturer and a moving company. Costs depend on a number of factors such as the size of your home and the distance it has to be transported. The moving company is responsible for obtaining all the necessary permits and licenses before transporting your home. You are responsible for obtaining mobile home insurance, which covers all liability and damages.

No matter if your home is new or used, if you don't own the land, you'll need to pay lot rent every month. The cost varies depending on where you are but you can expect to pay anywhere between $200 to $800 per month.

Who Buys Them?

The average buyer is either a first-time homeowner or a landowner. First time homebuyers prefer mobile homes since they are cheaper than a traditional home. The per-square-foot price is much lower, which means they get more house for their money. A mobile home's lower cost also means that saving a down payment is much easier. This makes homeownership a distinct possibility for many people that may not have had that opportunity otherwise.

The second type of mobile home buyer is a landowner. These people have money in the bank but their circumstances dictate a mobile home purchase. For example, the landowner might not want to commit to a fully built home on their land since it might reduce the number of people who would be interested in purchasing the land from them in the future. Let's say the land is adjacent to a ranch. The ranch owner might be interested in purchasing it in the future. The presence of a permanent home on the land means they would need to incur demolition costs that would reduce the selling price.

Placing a mobile home on the property is a much better bet. The landowner can lease the home to earn rent or live in it themselves. When the time comes to sell it, they can simply move the home elsewhere and sell the land as-is. Installing a mobile home also makes a lot of sense if the land is oddly shaped. You'll often see this in suburban areas where a patch of land between two existing structures exists.

These plots are too small and impractical for a fully-built home. It's far better to install a mobile home on the land and earn rent from it. A smaller subset of owners happen to be those who transport their homes to new locations every five years or so. They love to travel and transporting a mobile home beats buying a new home each time they move.

Advantages of Mobile Homes

Now that you know what mobile homes are, what are their advantages?

Lower Competition

Competition is an important factor you need to take into account when getting into real estate investing. The average beginner normally tries to flip or wholesale houses first. They think that it will be easy because they've been watching the TV stars on HGTV do it for the last 5 years. What they don't realize is that lots of people have that exact same idea! Residential real estate investors face a ton of competition from people who are investing full time and have much deeper pockets. They are also met with competition from other new investors who are willing to *just buy a deal*, even if it's not a smart one.

This isn't really the case with mobile home investing. For starters, they're basically invisible to most residential investors. They avoid mobile home parks like the plague, even if there is a cheap FSBO (for sale by owner) home there that can be fixed up with minor work and rented out for their target cashflow. Not to mention, many are scared of talking with the park managers to ensure that they can invest in that mobile home park and would rather skip it altogether.

New and experienced investors alike just aren't as interested in exploring the idea of investing in mobile homes. That means the market is less saturated and leads to a greater chance of success for those willing to take the plunge.

Lower Costs

Since mobile homes are so cheap, you don't need as large of a down payment to finance them.

The average single family home costs around $200,000. Single family homes are your average suburban house, with a lawn and a garage. A bank will usually expect you to pay 20% of the price as a down payment before they lend you the money to buy the property.

Twenty percent of $200,000 is $40,000. Once this is done, you'll need to pay monthly installments to service your loan. People usually opt to pay their loan back over 30 years since this reduces their monthly payments to a manageable $400-$800 range. The amount depends on the interest rate they receive but this is the typical target. Even though it's manageable, the average homebuyer is going to be in debt for 30 years. That's almost literally a lifetime!

A suburban homeowner typically buys a house when they're 28-30 years old. This means they'll fully own their property when they're 58-60, assuming they don't sell their home or ask for a deferral from their bank.

With mobile homes, your costs are much lower. The average new single-wide costs $51,000 and the average new double-wide costs $96,000[8]. You can buy even more expensive homes (called multi-wides or triple-wides) but these normally don't make sense from an investment perspective.

That means if you were to ignore my advice to buy used and opt to purchase a brand mobile home, you would need a maximum of $20,000 for a down payment. The rent you would earn from a mobile home is very similar to what you would earn from a traditional property so you could potentially afford to put more into the mortgage every month.

Good Demand

Here's the thing about mobile homes: They're not a sexy investment. You can't point to your first mobile home investment and expect people to understand that you're building a cashflow empire here. It's not like owning the Empire State Building or even a fancy mansion in Beverly Hills. In fact, most people might see it as the Walmart of real estate investments. However, what a lot of your friends, family, and other investors might not realize is that investing in Walmart is a smart move!

Walmart is a recession-proof business. In good times, they do well since everyone wants low-priced groceries. During bad times they do even better because people *need* low-priced groceries. This is exactly how mobile homes work as well! During good times, you'll have steady demand because there are always people in need of a place to live who don't have fantastic jobs. During bad times, you'll have even more demand since people will need cheaper housing options.

Your first few homes might not feel sexy, but once that money starts rolling in, you won't care. Let the other investors ego-invest while you invest wisely.

Low Turnover

This book is not just about rentals, but renting is one of the three main strategies you can use. As with any rental, in order to make money, you need to find people to rent your property! Turnover is a really big deal when it comes to renting out properties because the less turnover you have, the more passive your investment is.

Turnover refers to the time it takes for a tenant to move out. If your average tenant only lives in your property for one year, you'll need to spend money and time advertising your rentals *every year*. That doesn't sound like much but from an operational perspective, it can be a lot. If you have a tenant move out, you need to find a new one, clean the property, and fix any damage (usually with their security deposit). It can be a lot of work to find a new tenant - work that is necessary and pressing but at the same time not really moving your business forward like finding another mobile home would.

The best rental investors find tenants who stick around for a long time. This is why single-family homes are in huge demand. The average SFH renter is a young family with young kids. They're more likely to stay put for longer because they want their kids to grow up around their friends and attend the same school. You might think mobile homes aren't going to attract such tenants, but you'd be wrong.

A lot depends on your location of course. As long as your location is good, the average mobile home tenant sticks around for much longer than someone who leases an apartment. This is because the mobile home tenant is looking for good value for their money. They don't have the cash to spend on expensive moves. As a result, they end up sticking to a good deal when they find one. Moving out of a house is just as much work as it is for the tenant - especially a tenant that has enough furniture to furnish a 5 bedroom mobile home!

Less Maintenance

Did you know that the average single-family property owner spends half their rental profit on maintenance each year? In contrast, the cost of mobile home maintenance is much lower. For starters, the mobile home was built in a climate controlled factory, so they are already built better than most houses on the market. Secondly, their plumbing and foundation is mostly all exposed underneath. So, what could amount to a costly repair in a single family home wouldn't be all that much in a mobile home.

Safe and Secure

Mobile homes in the U.S. are manufactured according to standards set by the Housing and Urban Development (HUD) department of the U.S. government. These standards are exacting and ensure that mobile homes can cope with the same weather conditions and wear and tear that traditional homes undergo.

Taxes

Mobile homes offer lower property taxes on average compared to stick-built homes because they are much less expensive and your taxes are determined by the value of the property. In some states, you might even pay no property tax!

Lower taxes means you have less overhead eating into your investment so your returns will be greater. And what little taxes you do have, you can normally write off anyway. This makes mobile homes an attractive investment opportunity.

Types of Ownership

There are six main ways you can go about owning a mobile home property and generating a return on your investment through mobile home investing.

Owning a Home and Not the Land

Typically, mobile homes are set up in mobile home parks. These parks are owned by an investor who rents out plots of land to mobile home owners. Usually, park owners take care of the grounds so it is less work for you or your tenant to maintain the home.

There are many pros to investing in mobile homes using this strategy. For starters, you don't have to come up with a huge amount of money to purchase a parcel of land, fit it with all of the necessary utilities, and sit on it until you find people to rent out your lots or mobile homes. All you have to do is find a mobile home that is for sale, speak with the park owner to make sure you can sublet it, and put a down payment on the mobile home. It is magnitudes cheaper and a great way to get started if you only have enough money for a down payment but want to generate cashflow.

The downside is that you're at the mercy of the park owner. If they decide to increase rental fees you'll have to raise your rent, pay out of your own pocket, or move your unit. If your park manager raises your lot rent, it's usually better to stay put and raise your tenant's rent when their year lease is up. Moving a mobile home is much more expensive than finding new renters.

As you can see, there's a trade-off here. You're gaining convenience but are giving up control of your property. You'll still own your structure but you will be paying lot rents as long as you want your structure to rest on this land. One thing you can do is use this method to amass some mobile homes before you purchase some of your own land and move them there. Speaking of…

THE INVISIBLE DEAL

Owning the Land and the Units

This is the best of both worlds and the way that Mark (my friend from the beginning) chose to invest in mobile homes. You control the land as well as the units placed on it. That means you can run your community how you please and charge whatever you'd like. This model gives you a lot of flexibility in regards to spacing homes on your property. If there's a high demand for mobile homes in your area, you can increase the number of homes on your property and make more money. In some counties, you might need to have your land officially subdivided to rent mobile homes. The process isn't hard, though it can be expensive. If you have the money for it, it is more than worth it. Imagine being able to fit 6 mobile homes per acre. You'd make a small fortune on even a 5-acre plot.

Remember my friend Mark? Well he just went with the county's default of one mobile home per acre. This allowed him to charge a little more for each mobile home because each of his renters had a huge yard. If you so choose, you can reduce the density of homes and charge higher rents for the better quality of life you'll provide your tenants. As with everything else, you'll need to run the numbers to check how viable this is for you. Sometimes, if you can fit 2-3 extra mobile homes on an acre, the reduced rent is actually better for your bottom line. However, there is always a point of diminishing returns, so keep that in mind as you try to think about how you will structure your mobile home park.

There are some downsides to be aware of. Since you are renting these mobile homes out, you are technically the landlord. You will be responsible for fixing anything that breaks in the homes. If the plumbing bursts or the roof starts leaking, it will be up to you to make sure that it is repaired, and it will more than likely come out of your pocket unless you can prove that your renter damaged it somehow. (We save for these inevitabilities in an account called "CAPEX". More on this later.)

You will also be responsible for making sure the lawn is maintained, collecting all of the rent and filing your taxes. You can, of course, outsource this to rent collection companies like cozy.co, or use Intuit Quickbooks to make your life easier. They're both extremely cost effective and very useful for new businesses.

If these two apps don't have enough features for you, you can hire a property manager and an accountant. Keep in mind these services will eat into your bottom line. For instance, a property management firm may charge you as much as 10% of the monthly rent and one month's worth of rent to fill a vacancy.

I'd say, when you're first starting out, it's worth it to manage your own mobile home park and taxes. It will teach you a lot about both and keep you from being ripped off by unscrupulous businesses. Besides, managing a park isn't really that time consuming until you have 10+ units and by then, a property management company will be an expense that is well worth paying for.

You can find great lawn services, property management companies and CPAs on Thumbtack or Angie's List. I like these two websites because you can see what others are saying about their service and decide if they sound like a good company to partner with. I would advise avoiding Yelp and Google Business because the reviews on those sites can be manipulated relatively easily.

Owning the Land but Not the Units

To mitigate some of the risks of the previous method, you could choose to lease plots of land to mobile home owners. This is by far the most passive way to invest in real estate. The only things you have to worry about are the lawn and the utility hook-ups.

Owning the land frees up a lot of your time. You can realistically be a long distance owner without having to worry about maintenance. There's no need for you to worry about theft or crime either. After all, you can't really steal or damage land in the same way that you might damage a mobile home.

The only disadvantage is that your cash flow will be lower than if you were to rent out the mobile homes as well. However, if your plot is large enough to accommodate three or four units, you have the potential to earn $1,500 to $2,000 every month for almost no work.

Owning the Land and Financing the Units

If you own the land but want to incentivize people to stay in your units for a long time, you can offer them financing. This is known as seller-financing, owner-financing, or "rent-to-own". It is extremely common practice among mobile home and land owners.

Your buyers would basically take a loan from you and secure the loan using their mobile home. Basically, you act as the bank in this case. As the bank, you can offer whatever terms you like however mobile home terms are normally 5-10 years for 4% to 8% interest.

These terms give you the benefit of compound interest which is basically the magic that makes loans profitable. Seller financing is an excellent way to set up a short term passive income stream. We'll talk about this concept in depth later.

Charging lot rent while you seller finance out the homes that go on them is a very common operating procedure for mobile home parks, so you won't have any trouble finding a park buyer if you need to exit early. You could sell them the land with the mobile home loans or you could just sell them the land while you keep the mobile home mortgage loans.

You can also try your hand at selling these mobile home loans on the secondary market but you will probably find that the pool of investors who choose to invest in mobile home mortgages is even smaller than the pool of investors who invest in mobile homes!

That said, flipping a mobile home and seller financing it out on your own land gives you three streams of income. The mortgage(temporary), the interest(temporary), and the lot rent(forever). That certainly isn't a bad strategy!

Land and Unit Financing

This method extends the seller-financing option to both the land and the unit as well. At the end of the loan term, you'll have sold both the land as well as the properties on it. Not every investor likes this method because you won't have money coming in ad infinitum. However, some investors are willing to make the tradeoff for the extra level of passivity! Since you are seller-financing the entire parcel, you literally have zero maintenance. All the yardwork, unit maintenance, and utilities are up to the deed holder. The income you will make from the interest and the mark up from improving the land will be more than enough to find new investments so you can continue to generate passive income.

Many hands-off investors like the fact that this is a truly passive investment and actually opt for this type of investing. You have guaranteed income each month and you know you won't have to spend any money at all to maintain it. One question that often comes up when people ask about this method is "What if the note holders stop paying?"

If the note holders stop paying, you have a variety of options. The most common is to foreclose on them and sell the property to someone else. That means you get whatever payments they had already paid and you get to resell the exact same piece of property to someone else who will make even more payments! The downside is that you do have to pay for and go through the foreclosure process but you will more than make up what you spend here.

Fixer-upper

If this is really the method you would like to go with, then you'll be surprised to hear that banks and credit unions will not help you finance these flip deals if they do not come with land. It can be challenging to find financing for mobile homes when they are in good condition so if they are in "flip" condition, you probably won't be able to find anyone outside of a hard money lender*** to help you finance it. The good news is that fixer-uppers are extremely cheap. Sometimes they can even be free!

Once you have purchased your investment, you'll need to pay for the flip. Sometimes, mobile homes won't cost a lot of money to flip, especially if you want to leverage your own time and talents to fix them up.

However, if you don't have the money to flip a mobile home, you can always use the holy grail of free investment money: Zero percent APR credit cards.

Zero percent APR credit cards are my favorite loan vehicle because not only am I racking up points (read free money), I also have a really long time to pay it back! When I apply for them, I get anywhere from $8000-$12000 of free money and 9-18 months to pay it back. Investing is all about leveraging your money, and this is the best way to leverage it.

Mobile home flips take an average of 3 months from start to finish. That gives more than enough time to pay it back.

Don't get sucked into the negative talk about using credit cards. Credit card debt is only bad if it is for personal expenses. If you are leveraging a 0% loan to invest in a safe asset class like real estate, you are thinking like an investor.

*** Hard money lenders will give you a loan that has a very high interest rate (8-16%) for a very short term (6-18 months). Most hard money lenders will give you money for both property and flip. Keep in mind, the more money you borrow, the more interest you will have to pay. An 8% loan is basically highway robbery so if you can avoid hard money lenders then I would highly suggest you do. I will give you a few ways you can make some money with almost no money of your own in this book so please check those out before you get yourself into an expensive loan.

2

THE THREE MOST PROFITABLE WAYS TO INVEST IN MOBILE HOMES

There are three ways you can earn money by investing in mobile homes: wholesaling, flipping, and renting. This chapter will be a cursory overview on how each of these methods works, who they are best for, and approximately how much money or time each might take.

Wholesaling

What is Wholesaling

Wholesaling is very simple on the outset. All you have to do to wholesale is find a property, put it under contract, then assign the contract to an end buyer for a small fee. That sounds simple enough, after all, isn't that what realtors do?

Not quite!

Unlike realtors who sign a contract that states *they will make a commission if they sell the property*, wholesalers sign a contract stating *they will buy the property*. I'll say that again, when you wholesale and you sign a contract saying that you "or the assignee" will purchase the property, you are on the hook. If you don't find an assignee, then you technically must buy the property.

On the flip side, since you are facilitating this deal, you get to set the sales price that the end buyer purchases the property for, which is also known as "investing in the spread". That means, as a wholesaler, you make whatever the difference is between buying the property and selling it. The thing is, you never actually buy it. You just assign your contract to another buyer for a higher price.

Wholesalers are an important part of the real estate investing ecosystem because their job is to do the hardest and most important function of real estate investing: finding deals. That definitely sounds easy on paper, but it can be much harder in practice. Lucky for us, finding mobile homes to wholesale is much easier than finding your typical stick-built home because there are far fewer investors trying to buy and sell mobile homes than there are single family home (SFH) investors.

Who Should Wholesale

A great wholesaler is patient, tenacious and a natural people-person. As a wholesaler, you will deal with a lot of rejection. After all, you're playing a numbers game! Not every property owner will want to sell and even if they do, they might not be motivated enough! That's why it's so important that you are able to handle rejection as a wholesaler. You'll get a lot of "No!"s before you get one "Yes!".

As a wholesaler, you need to hustle and work really hard to make deals work, but when you do, the payouts can be enormous! Imagine having zero dollars one day and having

10 grand the next. That is more than possible if you choose to wholesale!

Many people who have no money to invest get started with wholesaling. They might wholesale every three and use the money they made from those deals to keep one. Some investors actually find that they like wholesaling and decide to make a business out of it!

Wholesaling is not particularly my favorite activity but if you're new to investing, my advice is to give it a try. If you find you don't like it then you can always pick up a few extra shifts at a part time job to save up for a down payment.

How does wholesaling work

Wholesalers try to find motivated sellers who are likely to let their property go for less than it is worth because they *just want it done*. Motivated sellers are usually one of the following:

1. They've been trying to sell the mobile home for 6+ months, but just can't seem to find a buyer. They are tired of paying the lot rent and other fees and just *want this thing gone* because they realize they are losing money with each passing month.
2. They inherited the property from one of their relatives and do not want to put any effort into selling it. They have had all of the expenses that come with a mobile home dropped in their lap and they *just want it gone*!
3. Something extremely terrible has happened in their life recently. Maybe they were laid off, maybe one of their kids got sick. At any rate, they can't afford to

live where they are living right now or maybe they just need to sell the mobile home to pay the unexpected expense. Time is of the essence and *they need to sell it now*!
4. They got a new job or their current company is moving them somewhere far away. They only have a few weeks to figure out how to wrap up their life here and move to the new location. They need to sell this mobile home now because it's cheaper just to sell it and buy a new one than it is to pack it all up and haul it across the country. They *need to sell it fast* so they have enough time and money to buy a new place to live!

Notice a trend with all of these sellers? They need to sell their mobile home *now!* Most of these motivated sellers would prefer to lose a little money on their home for the convenience of just having it gone! These are the types of sellers you will be targeting as a wholesaler because they will be willing to sell you their property at a price that will allow you to turn a pretty good profit.

Every property's sale and purchase agreement has an option called "assignment". This is literally a single line in the agreement which says that the buyer mentioned in the agreement can assign the contract to someone else. The seller signs the agreement with the wholesaler who then assigns it to the buyer. Let's look at some numbers to see how everyone benefits in such a deal.

Let's say the seller and wholesaler negotiate with one another and agree on a price of $10,000 for the property. The wholesaler goes to the buyer and negotiates a price of $20,000 with them. Once the buyer agrees, the wholesaler and seller sign the contract.

The wholesaler transfers $10,000 to the seller and keeps the remainder. The property's title passes to the buyer and everyone's happy. There will be a minor $300 for a traveling notary (Who needs to be a disinterested party who is there to witness a signature on legal documents. I.e. you can't get your notary license and do this yourself!) but this can be easily taken out of the seller's profits, as is the standard operating procedure when selling real estate.

Wholesalers aren't real estate professionals and this places certain restrictions on them. Each state has different requirements. You'll need to check with your local real estate investing club to see what the case is in your area. Go to Meetup.com and search for real estate investing clubs in the area you would like to invest in. Post a question on the forums (or search for a previous post) to determine how wholesaling works in your state. Avoid asking a realtor because they will likely tell you it is illegal, even if that isn't true.

Wholesaling can be a little more difficult in the beginning than other methods because you'll have to juggle a few balls at once to make deals work. Not only do you have to find a motivated seller, you will also have to find a buyer that wants to buy your property!

Don't let this scare you away. You can always write a contingency into the contract stating that you can terminate the deal at any time, for any reason. If you can't find a buyer in time, then you can either ask for an extension or exercise this contingency and terminate the contract.

Keep in mind that wholesaling is a people business. It will be a little slow in the beginning because you won't know the mobile home real estate investors in the area, won't have a reputation, and won't have a large buyer's list. However, as you continue to do more and more deals, you will know more and more people. This has a kind of feedback loop effect that will be very good for you and your business! The more people who know you wholesale, the more deals will come your way, especially if you take care of your buyers and sellers. Make sure you always treat them cordially and explain everything thoroughly.

In this age, you can do a lot of the activities you need to find and sell mobile homes over the internet. Unless you can convince your prospective seller to do everything digitally, you will eventually need to drive to whatever mobile home you are trying to buy. That said, a lot of the preliminary items can be done from the comfort of your own home, using apps like Facebook Marketplace or Craigslist. It also helps if you are local to the area in which you are trying to source deals because driving through the mobile home parks and putting up bandit signs (those small real estate signs you see posted along a road) are great ways to cheaply advertise yourself to motivated sellers.

Pros

The biggest pro for me is that wholesaling literally allows you to turn a few hundred dollars into thousands in a relatively short amount of time. All you need to do is connect a buyer and a seller. As long as the property meets the buyer's requirements and they have the cash, you have a deal. You might find yourself earning a few thousand dollars for a week's worth of work without putting your own money at risk. That's an almost infinite return on your investment (ROI) because the only money that you spend is whatever you choose to spend on advertising. None of your money actually goes into the deal being made.

Another huge pro, and something that speeds up the deal process, is that you don't have to undergo any credit checks. Mobile home parks require credit approval, but since you aren't planning on taking possession, you can skip this step. Note that your buyer will most likely have to undergo this process, so make sure there is a clause in the contract that states you can break the contract if the buyer does not pass the park's credit check.

Finding a good deal is often the hardest part of investing in real estate, so be warned that wholesaling is tough! However, if you don't have any money and are serious about investing, it is by far the cheapest way to start. I've seen lots of mobile home wholesalers make well over $10,000 on a deal. Of course, your success will depend on how good you are at negotiating with the seller.

As they say, you make all your money when you buy!

As a new investor, you should expect your first deal to break even, which is **not** a bad thing. I'll let you in on a secret that other real estate investors don't want to tell you… Your first deal isn't actually about making money, it's about teaching you how wholesaling works. Doing one deal is better than reading about a million. You'll gain a lot of the knowledge you need to succeed and I can almost guarantee you that the next deal will be 100x easier and more profitable!

Cons

By far the biggest con is the time it will take to find a deal. The first deal might take you a few months to find. More than likely, you'll go see 10 mobile homes before you actually end up finding a motivated seller who is willing to sell you the home for a price that will be profitable to you. Do not get discouraged.

Wholesaling is one of the harder ways to invest in real estate because finding the deal (the very first step!) is always the hardest step! That's why when real estate investors find a really good wholesaler, they hold them tight and treat them well.

Once you find a deal, the clock really starts ticking. You need to find a buyer who is interested in the home you bought and will pay a price that is profitable for you, all before it's time to sign! Rarely, but more so when you are first starting out, you might not be able to find a buyer in time and you will be forced to either ask for an extension or terminate the contract. The best way to mitigate this is to start making a list of potential buyers before you even have a deal. We'll go over just how to do that later on.

The second best way to mitigate the termination risk is to set your closing date as far out as the sellers will allow. Closings usually take a long time anyway, so it's not uncommon for two to three months to pass before a normal deal is closed. If you do end up finding a buyer and are in a hurry to make some money, you can always ask the seller to amend the original contract so that you can close sooner. If they are fine closing sooner, great! If they aren't, then no problem, you have both your buyer and seller locked in and you can relax until closing!

If you really can't find a buyer, and you've already asked for one extension, you can terminate the contract. Do not panic if this happens because, again, when you create your contract you should include a clause that allows you to terminate any time up until the closing date for any reason.

This will make it legal for you to break the contract and not lose any money except for your earnest fee (if your state requires one, you should put a fee of $20 down to secure your investment, so at worst, you will lose $20). Being unable to find a buyer is not ideal, but it's not the end of the world. If you have to terminate a deal or two in the beginning, it won't really damage your reputation because you're relatively unknown anyway. Just don't make a habit out of it! Besides, if you go through all the work of finding a deal but can't find a way to sell, you'll be working for free and who wants that?!

Making It A Game (How to avoid getting discouraged)

If you've never been in sales before then you probably don't know how to handle all of the mental strain that comes with constant rejection. If you have been in sales, then welcome back!

Luckily, there are a few things you can do to make wholesaling a little bit less draining. First, you need to separate out your leads into three categories. The first category is every call that connected. The second category is everyone who said yes to an appointment. The third category is everyone you bought a home from.

The First Category – Every Connected Call

You should be striving to make x amount of calls each day. Whether that's one or one hundred is up to you and how much time you have, but you need to make sure you set a number and stick with it. Let's just say that you decide you're going to make 10 calls each day.

For each of those calls, you keep track of everyone who picked up. This is your only success metric for this category, how many people picked up.

Let's say you called 100 people and out of those 100, only ten picked up or called you back. You have a success rate of 10%!

The Second Category – Everyone Who Said Yes to an Appointment

Now, that you have your measure of success from the first category, you can use that as the baseline for your second category. You take all the people who picked up in your first category and count how many of them agreed to an appointment.

Let's say you had ten people pick up. Out of those ten, two of them decided that you had a great offer. Your success rate is 20%!

The Third Category – Everyone Who Sold You Their Home

You now have two people who said yes to an appointment. You go to each of their homes, appraise them with the checklist companion I included in the link at the beginning of this book.

Out of those two people, one of them decided that they would accept your deal. That's a success rate of 50%!

Keeping track of these categories is an excellent way to keep your spirits up. When you start to see things like people hanging up on you as a success, then you stop caring about people hanging up on you.

The Secret Fourth Category – Every Call Pays You

The last strategy you can use to avoid getting discouraged is to think about every call as a call that paid you. Let's say you make $20,000 in one month. In that same month, you made 200 calls. To find out how much each call paid you, you divide how much you made by the number of calls you made. So, $20,000 / 200 = $100. Each call paid you $100.

You see, people are funny. Each individual person might be different, but when you start to look at people on the whole, you begin to see patterns. That's the difference between a micro analysis (analyzing one person) and a macro analysis (analyzing all people as a whole). When you look at people on a macro scale, you can start generalizing.

So, if you made $100 per call this month, you can expect to make $100 per call next month. If you make twice the calls, you make twice the money!

Of course, as you get better at calling, you will make more money per call or take less time per call (so you can call more). But, if you just need a little encouragement in the short term, thinking about things in the terms of dollars/call is a great trick!

Flipping

What is Flipping

Flipping is the process of buying a property that is in a state of disrepair, fixing it, and then selling it for a higher price.

Who Should Flip

Mobile homes are obviously much easier to flip than residential homes because they are raised off the ground (easy access to pipes and foundation) and they are less complicated so fewer things can break.

If you have an eye for design, are a natural project manager and have a couple thousand dollars, then flipping might be right up your alley! Construction knowledge is also a plus when it comes to flipping because you will need to accurately estimate how much money it will take to turn your run down trailer into a five-star mobile home.

If you are interested in flipping, I would advise you to have at least $5000 saved up. You will either need this for a down payment or to buy the mobile home outright. More than likely, you're going to have to seller-finance the flip, if you can find a loan at all. Banks don't like making loans on decrepit properties.

I also recommend you have a credit score above 680 because you will likely need to take out some kind of loan to pay for repairs. A higher credit score definitely gives you better rates, but 680 should do the job just fine.

Flipping is also great for investors who want to get paid large lump sums and have some time on their hands to manage contractors and visit the job site. If you aren't interested in becoming a landlord but still want to make money from mobile homes, then flipping is your best bet! You can even leverage wholesalers in your area if you find that you don't like hustling to find the deals yourself!

How to Flip

When it comes to flipping, you stand to earn a higher return with mobile homes because they depreciate very quickly. This makes it easy to find bargains on old homes that need what appears to be a lot of work but isn't really.

Finding a mobile home

As for finding mobile homes, your first one might require a little bit of effort. You should try to find wholesalers and realtors who also deal in mobile homes because they will do a lot of the hard work of finding deals for you. The downside is that there are few wholesalers and realtors who deal in mobile homes, so it may be hard to find them! Not to worry, there are many ways to find mobile homes that we will detail later.

Since you are flipping, the mobile homes that you are interested in will likely be marked way down already. And, while you want to get the best deal you can, you probably don't need to worry about squeezing every dollar out of the seller. Instead, think about out how to cheaply add value to the mobile home.

This won't happen overnight of course. It takes time to successfully find a good property for a flip. You'll need to conduct thorough research into prices in your area and how much you can reasonably resell your property for. However, the work is worth it. You will be undertaking more risk than a wholesaler but the rewards are much more substantial.

Financing your flip

There are two distinct things you will need to finance when you want to flip a mobile home: the property and the "upgrades". I put upgrades in quotes because sometimes you're not even upgrading the house, you're straight up fixing it!

There are a few different ways you can get money to purchase the property:

1. The best option is to ask the seller if they would be willing to seller-finance. This is a great way to invest in the spread because you might just get away with paying $1000 down payment and a few hundred bucks a month in holding fees for a mobile home that the seller wants $5000 for. (Of course, you'll pay them the remainder of the balance once you get paid for your flip, you just have to come up with less money on the front end.)
2. The next best option is to save up enough cash to finance the actual purchase of the property yourself. I don't often suggest you save cash for any real estate purchase because I am a big believer in leveraging debt, but with ratted out mobile homes, cash is a great option. It's hard enough to find financing for detached mobile homes in good condition!
3. If the previous two options don't work for you, you'll have to find the money some other way. Whether that's through a hard money loan, a personal loan

from your bank or crowdsourcing the funds from your friends, that's up to you. None of them are necessarily better than the other.

There are a few different ways you can get money for a flip:

1. My favorite (and the best!) was is to apply for a 0% APR credit card***. This usually results in a 0% interest rate for the first eight to 18 months which is enough time to flip that mobile home three times, let alone once.
2. The next best option is to take out a personal loan from your bank. This usually results in a 3%-8% interest rate for a short term. This is the middle of the road option that will work well for you if you have an outstanding credit score.
3. The least best option is to borrow from a hard money lender. This usually results in an 8% to 12% interest rate for a 6 to 18 month term. It's the bottom of the barrel option, in my opinion.
4. If you don't have very good credit and you can't get a loan through these methods, you can also raise money from your friends and family, offer to partner with someone in your REIA (Real Estate Investment Association) club or, in the worst case scenario, borrow from your 401k.
5. Of course, an honorable mention for cash. If you would like to use money lying around to flip your mobile home, then that is up to you but you could be using that money as a downpayment to purchase more flips or rentals!

***As I said earlier, my personal favorite method is using 0% APR credit cards. Since you're repaying it before the term is up, it's basically free money. You can find offers for these cards on CreditKarma.com.

Estimating repair costs

Like any other flip, the most crucial part of making a flip work is estimating repair costs. No matter how much you read about repair costs, you won't be an expert until you've flipped a few homes. Why? Because each area has a different cost for materials and each contractor/handyman has a different cost for labor. However, you can get a back of the napkin estimate by fully inspecting the home and calling around to ask for bids. I give an inspection worksheet at www.MateosMobiles.com/mobiles.

Mobile homes are smaller than the average single-family home. There are no underground maintenance issues such as the sump or having to worry about basements being flooded. As long as the frame is in good condition, most of the repairs you'll need to carry out might look bad but are usually fairly cosmetic.

Once you've walked through the mobile home and discovered what might need to be repaired, you should do a back of the napkin estimate using a calculator. Keep in mind, it's not impossible to spend too much when you purchase a mobile home but it is a lot harder than SFH.

Mobile homes are not very complicated so not much can go wrong. I say all this to help you understand that if you end up missing a repair in your estimate (you likely will) it probably won't set you back very much.

The best advice I ever got was to look at my first deal as an on-the-job learning experience. When you do your first flip, you'll learn more from any mistake you make than you ever could from reading a book or buying a program. There is nothing like hands on experience, especially if it causes you to miss out on a little bit of profit!

Purchasing the home

The next step is to do a preliminary negotiation. After you know what needs to be repaired, you can use that information to negotiate the price down. The less you spend on purchasing the mobile home, the more money you will make when you sell it. If you are buying this mobile home from a wholesaler, then more than likely they will not negotiate with you. However, if you found this deal yourself you will have quite a bit of wiggle room, especially if the owner thinks the mobile home is in a severe state of disrepair or just really wants to sell it (see my four motivated sellers in the wholesale section).

If you and the seller have decided on a preliminary price, you can sign a contract. Make sure this contract has the same contingency clause as the wholesale contract, so you can terminate for any reason up until the closing date.

If you put the mobile home under contract, chances are that you really want to purchase it. For your first 10 or so flips, you should spend the extra money to get it inspected.

Hiring a good inspector is a great investment because they can tell you definitively what needs to be fixed. If the mobile home does have structural damage, this will save you thousands of dollars because you can simply abandon the deal all for the price of your $20 earnest fee. An inspector's report can also help you negotiate the price down even further before closing if there are extensive repairs that you didn't catch on your initial walkthrough.

If you want to stop spending money on inspectors, you should follow them around and ask them questions as they inspect your mobile home. Once you've seen this done a few times, you'll more than likely be able to do it yourself! I will give you a guide about what to look out for later in the book so that you'll already have a good foundation.

Flipping the home

Once the inspection is done, you can start to collect bids from general contractors in your area. If the mobile home only has cosmetic issues, you can opt to either fix them yourself or hire a handyman. Anything beyond cosmetic will likely require a general contractor. You can find both of these professionals at your REIA club, on Thumbtack.com or on Angie's List.

Depending on the amount of damage and the speed of your general contractor or handyman, a flip could take anywhere from one to six months. When you get your contract together for the GCs (General Contractors), separate the work out into three draws.

That basically means you're going to group the work into three sections and pay the contractor as they complete each one. We'll go over this more in detail in Chapters 4 and 5. Make sure you get quotes from several contractors/handymen before you sign on with one. These guys are mostly honest but every now and then you'll find one that is willing to take advantage of new investors.

THE INVISIBLE DEAL

Selling the home

Once you flip it, selling is the easy part! I'll teach you how to leverage free and mostly-free apps so you can sell your flip quickly and for a nice profit!

Pros

Flipping is a quick way for investors to turn a huge profit. It isn't unheard of to earn a return within three months. This is a pretty short period of time to earn five figures in returns. For example, if you buy a used home for $15,000, spend another $15,000 refurbishing it, and sell it for $80,000 you've earned a $50,000 profit. Not bad for a few months' work!

Another pro is that you are reducing waste! If you like recycling, then flipping will be really rewarding for you because you are taking something that was about to be thrown away and turning it into something someone will live in.

Cons

Flipping is a rewarding method of earning a return but it's risky as well. Your repair estimates are likely to be wrong and you might even run into a few crooked contractors. I will do everything I can to help you avoid these issues, but it does happen.

It can also take a lot of patience to find a property worth purchasing and flipping. Lots of new investors are extremely impatient because they underestimate the amount of effort and luck that goes into finding a good deal. This is especially true about flips! Don't fall into that trap. Trust your gut and practice patience. A great deal will come your way eventually.

Rentals

What is Renting

Investing in mobile homes as rental properties is a versatile way of earning money from your investment. Earlier on, in Chapter 1, I detailed all of the different ways you could make money from renting out mobile homes (including a few ways you could make money by renting out plots of land). Before we dive into the nuances of each method, we need to first examine whether mobile homes are real estate or not.

For starters, the land that the mobile home rests on is considered real estate. The mobile home itself can be considered either personal property or real estate. Like many things in real estate different countries (and even states!) deal with this question in different ways. In some areas, mobile homes are always considered real estate. In others, if the home and land are owned by different people, the home is considered real estate. If both land and the home are owned by the same person, the home might be considered personal property[9].

The reason this distinction is important is because personal property and real estate are taxed differently, at least in the USA. For instance, in the USA mobile homes that are used to earn rental income are considered real estate and the standard 27.5 years depreciation rule applies to them. Depreciation is when the value of a property decreases over time and can be used to write off some of your taxes.

This has major implications for real estate investors. Let's say the value of your mobile home is $90,000. You'll have to write this down to zero over the course of 27.5 years. This means you'll reduce this value by (90000/27.5) or $3,272 every year. You can deduct this amount of money from your taxes each year.

If you live in a different country, your country likely has something similar to this. Contact an accountant or read up on its laws in order to get the full picture!

Who Should Rent

Renting out mobile homes is my favorite method of mobile home investing. If you want to rent out mobile homes, all you have to do is find a mobile home that will make more in rental income than what it takes to own it.

If you have $5,000-$10,000, don't want to spend a lot of time sourcing deals, have a decent credit score (680+) and want to create years of cashflow, then renting out mobile homes is a great choice!

How to Rent

There are two ways in which you can rent out your property. The first situation is if you own the land and the home. In this case, working out the numbers is quite straightforward. You earn rental income from your tenant and that's it. The second scenario is a little more complex. In this scenario, you own the home but not the land on which it sits.

In this case you'll be responsible for paying the lot fee to the landowner from the rent you collect from your tenants. You'll also have to deal with more paperwork and rules as well. Some mobile home parks don't approve of owners renting their homes out to tenants. Others will want to thoroughly vet the people you are considering before they sign a rental agreement. Some parks don't care as long as your renters are quiet, good Samaritans.

Make sure you check out all of your prospective park's rules before deciding to invest in a property. You want to make friends with the mobile home park managers and follow all their rules, guidelines and regulations.

If you prove that you aren't going to cause trouble, the park managers will be more likely to help you! Sometimes, they'll even let you know when a mobile home comes up for sale on their property or when a lot has become available. This is another lead-generation technique you can use and one that scales as you own more mobile homes in more parks.

That said, the actual rental process is fairly straightforward. If you're trying to find individual mobile homes in park, here is some general guidance:

1. You find a mobile home that is for sale.
2. You do some due diligence to figure out if the area is a good area. I'll tell you how to do this in detail later.
3. Once you've determined if it's a good area, you do an analysis on how much rent that home will earn each month vs how much you will have to spend each month to own it.
4. If you determine that you can make money on that mobile home, then you purchase it.
5. Once you've bought it, you seek renters.

6. After you have a pool of renters, you vet them. You should make sure they have decent credit scores, no criminal record, and haven't been evicted before.
7. You sign a lease.
8. Once they've signed a lease, you automate as much as you can. I like cozy.co (an online system that will easily allow them to pay you, make maintenance requests, etc).

If you are trying to rent out a mobile home on land, then the process is very similar except you own the land, so you will set your own standards on who can rent it.

CAPEX

Capex is an important expense that many new landlords forget to account for. When you own a property, you are responsible for fixing it when things break and filling vacancies. In either case, you usually need some money to pay for the repairs or pay holding costs. That's where CAPEX comes in.

Each time you receive rent, you should save between five and ten percent in case of emergency. I like to open a savings account in my business's name and dump all of the capex there, but what you do with it is up to you.

At a minimum, I like to save 6 months worth of holding costs or $5000 in my capex savings account (whichever is greater). That way if something absolutely abysmal happens, I have at least six months to figure out how to fix it. Sure, it could be that selling the mobile home is the best course of action, but if I have six months worth of holding costs in there then I don't have to scramble to sell it. I can take my time and find a buyer who will pay me what I think it is worth.

Pros

Mobile homes don't cost much so you recover your investment very quickly. I have seen mobile homes rent for about the price of an apartment. For instance, in my area, a 2-bedroom, 1-bathroom apartment rents for $1300. A double-wide with no lawn and 5 bedrooms and 3 baths rents for about that much. It's a great deal for your renters and a great opportunity for cashflow for you!

Another pro is if you have vacant land you'll find that putting a mobile home on it is far easier and faster than building a structure on it. Even if you put a modular home on it, you will still find that it is much faster to recover your investment and start taking in major cashflow than investing in a SFH.

Cons

No matter how much care you put into a mobile home, it will depreciate over time. That is why it's crucial that you buy a used mobile home since this reduces your upfront expenses and gets your cashflow going within a few years of purchasing it instead of 30 years later.

Think of it like buying a car. It's going to depreciate so you might as well reduce your upfront expense. However, you don't want to buy a car that's going to break down all the time. The key is to find balance. Some investors struggle with this and end up paying too much. Now, mobile homes are not a very high stakes investment, so you will probably recover your initial investment. It'll just take you longer than if you hadn't made that mistake in the first place.

Lot rents present a hurdle for the rental investor. This is because they're due no matter what. Often, lot rents eat up a significant portion of the rent you earn from your tenants.

Maintenance is also a concern for landlords. Mobile homes need some maintenance and many investors outsource this to the tenants. While a good tenant will take care of your home, you'll still need to perform structural maintenance on the property to make sure the frame remains solid. We will account for this with a monthly savings account called capex when we calculate your ROI later on.

If you'd like to get a sneak peek at this calculator now, you can go to www.MateosMobiles.com/mobiles.

PART 2

THE ULTIMATE STEP-BY-STEP GUIDE TO FINDING YOUR FIRST INVESTMENT THIS MONTH

3

STEP 1: HOW TO FIND A PROFITABLE DEAL

The only surefire way of making money on mobile homes is to find and purchase great deals.

When I say great deals, I mean mobile homes that are priced far below what they are worth, or will be worth once you add value. The lower the price you pay for your investment, the greater your return will be.

Duh!

So how do you find these great deals?

Finding a great deal is the hardest job for any new real estate investor. First off, you don't have the infrastructure set up so that they just "fall in your lap". Second, you probably don't even know what a great deal looks like. You might think you do, but chances are, if you haven't invested before, you don't.

Thankfully, through a combination of reading this book and putting yourself out there, you will learn!

This chapter is mainly focused on setting up your deal finding infrastructure. We will go over several methods that many investors use to find mobile home deals. Many of them are well known so I wouldn't be surprised if you are familiar with them already! Some people might complain that these methods are the same old methods you hear about everywhere. *Where's the new stuff? You know, that stuff nobody uses?!*

I'll tell you where the new stuff nobody uses is. It's in the garbage! People don't use tactics that don't work. I only tell my new investors about methods that actually work. I leave that experimental garbage out. Nothing is new under the sun!

That said, all of these methods do work, but not all of them work for every investor in every area. You might find that you really enjoy driving for dollars or you may think that mailing campaigns are well worth the money. It all depends on how much money or time you have and what other investors (if there are any) are doing in your area. I suggest you choose two marketing techniques and give them a solid try for 3-6 months. I'd caution you against setting up more than two at a time because it might make you feel overwhelmed.

The 5 Best Deal Finding Methods

Driving for Dollars

This is the tried and true method of finding great real estate deals. Why do I know this? Because investors are willing to pay bird dogs (people who find deals and sell the lead to an investor) $100 for every deal they find, and lots of bird dogs make their living finding deals (and eventually investing themselves)!

Now, driving for dollars is exactly what it sounds like.

Step 1: You need to find mobile home parks in your area.
Step 2: You ask the park manager if they know of any mobile homes for sale.
Step 3: You drive through the mobile home park looking for FSBO signs.

Sounds easy enough, right?

Finding Mobile Home Parks

I don't call this book *The Invisible Deal* for nothing! You can drive through an area 20 times and not realize you're driving near the entrance of a mobile home park. But as soon as you start thinking about investing in mobile homes - wham! There they all are.

However, driving around town with your newfound mobile home spidey sense isn't a very efficient use of time, so we're going to use the internet instead! It's very important to locate and plan out your route when you're driving for dollars. First off, it saves you gas (the only monetary expense for this marketing method). Second, it saves you time (which is a more important expense than almost any amount of money).

If you live in a big city, you may need to drive to the outskirts to find mobile home parks. Feel free to download all of my audiobooks and block out an entire Saturday to go drive as many of these parks as you can! Remember, this is a numbers game. Not every FSBO is going to be a homerun, some of them are not going to be good deals for you, so you need to find as many as possible.

Go to Google and type in "Mobile Home Parks in <Your City>".

A map pack should come up. Click on it. That should show you where all of the mobile home parks are in your area. Some of these will be RV parks. If you aren't looking to rent out vacation rentals in RV parks, then you can ignore them. To figure out if they are RV parks, you just need to look at the pictures. If none of the pictures show mobile homes, then it means it's a waste of time to canvas that park.

Creating Your Route

Now that you've found a few mobile home parks, you can create a route. This is as simple as going to Google and typing in all of the addresses from the mobile home parks you found. Then, dragging and dropping them until you have them in a logical order.

Driving for Dollars

Now that you know where you will be driving, schedule out a day in which you're going to drive through them! When you drive through these parks, first visit the management center (if they have one) and ask if they know of any for sale. Write down all of the addresses they tell you. Then, drive through the park and look for "For Sale By Owner" signs. Write down all of those addresses, take a picture of the mobile home and note the phone number on the sign.

Contacting the FSBO owners

The next day, call all of the FSBO owners. I have an exact script of what you should say at www.MateosMobiles.com/mobiles.

Other Advice

Try to enjoy the process of driving for dollars. You shouldn't feel like you *need* to find a deal *or else you'll die*. You should instead look at it as an adventure. When I used to drive for dollars, I'd always be sure to have an audiobook or podcast playing in the background so that I could learn while looking for deals. And remember, you won't always be driving for dollars, you're just driving for dollars until you can automate your deal funnel.

The key to automation is to build relationships as you drive around a neighborhood. Give people your business card and let them know if they find a deal that works out, you'll give them $100. Go into convenience stores, and other local areas. Talk to the managers. Get their phone numbers if you can and keep checking back in periodically. If you remind people that you exist about once every three months, they'll start to think of you when they notice a deal nearby. Even if it's a FSBO sign, let them know that if you close on that deal they'll make $100!

It can be disheartening at first and you might wonder whether you're just wasting gas, but keep at it and remember that you never know where a good lead might come from.

When you are talking with a park manager, you can also ask if it is ok for you to put up a poster in the clubhouse. Many of these mobile home parks have a place where residents pass by or gather on a semi-regular basis. If you place a poster with your contact information claiming that you buy mobile homes quickly, as-is, people will contact you!

This is all about setting up a deal pipeline. Plant the seeds now so you can reap your harvest later!

Bandit Signs

Have you seen little yellow or white signs in the ground or on light poles in your town? Those are bandit signs! They're cheap to make and basically free to put out. If you are going to drive for dollars, I suggest you make a few bandit signs as well and put them out near the entrance of the mobile home parks. Even if you don't have time to actually drive through the parks, bandit signs are a great second option.

You can get signs printed and fixed to frames that you can post on the sides of major intersections. Yellow boards cost more than white ones and obviously printing a sign is going to cost you more than handwriting one.

When you look for places to put your signs, you should favor major traffic intersections. This is a bit of a gray area, but technically speaking, you can post these signs on the side of the road. Fair warning, they may be removed by the city or a homeless person eventually, but I have a few tricks up my sleeve to make that less likely.

In terms of size, larger ones are easier to see. These signs will cost you more to make but they'll also attract more attention. When choosing your locations, remember that traffic isn't your only consideration. Drivers need to be able to stop and safely read your sign. Sticking a bandit sign on the highway isn't going to work. This is why traffic intersections are a great idea. It gives people enough time to write down your phone number before the light turns green.

The key to these signs is simplicity! Ignore the feeling that you need to try to cram in as many words as possible. It is even fine to ignore grammar so long as you get your point across.

We Buy Mobile Homes
Call xxx-xxx-xxxx
FAST, As-is, For Cash

A sign to attract Sellers

> Mobile Home for Sale!
>
> Call xxx-xxx-xxxx
>
> 3 bed/2 bath great condition

A sign to attract Buyers

A few key points about these signs. Don't try to be different than everyone else! You aren't going to trick anyone into calling you by putting something fancy on your sign. These simple bandit signs that just get the point across are clear, concise, and take almost no time to write yourself.

Also, you'll notice that I'm assuming you'll leave a phone number on the sign for prospects to call. This number doesn't have to be your personal phone number. In fact, I recommend against leaving your personal number on a public sign. Who knows who might decide to call you at four in the morning?

Instead, get yourself a Google Voice number. This will forward calls to your phone and you can even have people leave voicemails there. A more robust paid option is to use RingCentral for $34.99 per month. You get unlimited texts, 1000 minutes, and several lines on their standard plan. The app works on iPhones and Android phones, so you don't need an entirely new phone. This also allows a separation of voicemails from personal and business and the cost can be expensed come tax season.

Another option is to leave an easy URL on your sign. People are tech savvy these days and might even prefer to visit a website instead of talking on the phone. On the website, you can set up a simple "landing page" where you ask for their email, their name, and their phone number. If they are selling a mobile home, you can also ask for the address, which makes it easier to do some due diligence before you get on the phone with them.

If you aren't tech savvy but like the idea of having a simple landing page, you can visit www.ScalableRealEstate.com and they will set one up for you.

Capturing their email address lets you market to them far beyond the initial screening. For both mobile home sellers and buyers, you can send them information about the market, neat articles on how to maintain their mobile home, and deals that you find on items for mobile home users. For sellers, you can send them the mobile homes that you are trying to sell. It's a quick and easy way to sell them with almost no effort.

For email marketing, I like using www.ActiveCampaign.com. It allows you to set up campaigns quickly and send emails to anyone who has opted in to receiving emails from you.

Lots of investors might wonder why they should go through all the trouble of marketing themselves online. It goes back to a marketing technique as old as marketing itself. That simple principle is if people don't remember who you are, they aren't going to remember to give you leads. If people don't trust you, they aren't going to sell your their house. It's that simple.

Leveraging the internet is a great way to remind prospective buyers and sellers that you exist and convince them that you are an expert. If they trust you and you remain at the forefront of your contacts' minds, then they'll get in touch with you down the road if they have a mobile home to sell (or if they want to buy one).

This advice goes for any phone number or email you capture. It's not just about placing a sign on the side of the road and waiting for people to call. You need a system to manage your leads, classify them, and store the relevant information of people who seem like genuine prospects.

Setting Up your Bandit Sign

There are two main ways to place your bandit signs. The first way is to purchase the bandit signs that stick in the ground. The next way is to buy just the sign portion of it and then fasten it to a light pole.

To fix it to a light pole, all you need is 2 screws and a drill. Reach up as high as you can and put the first screw in the top center. Then, put the second screw halfway between the middle and the bottom of the sign. See the "x" below.

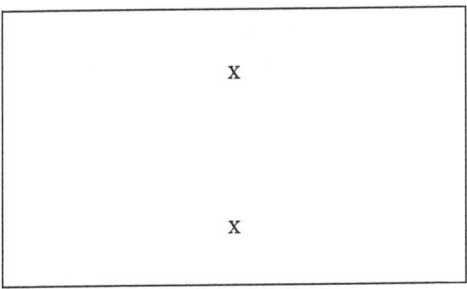

Where to put screws on a Bandit Sign

I have put together a shopping cart of everything you need for bandit signs at www.MateosMobiles.com/mobiles-leads. From a drill to screws to the sign itself, you can buy all the materials I use there.

After you have your bandit signs, you will need to do a few things. First, if you only had your message printed on one side, you need to draw a big X on the back. This X needs to go from one corner to the other. This is to prevent homeless people from stealing your signs. They can't write their messages on the back if there's a big black X.

Remember! Place them at busy intersections near the mobile home parks as high up on a light pole as you can reach. Bring a drill for quick install!

If you find that your signs are being stolen fairly frequently, you can go to the second method of attaching them to light poles - zip ties! Punch a hole on both sides of your sign, wrap it around the light pole, and then stick a zip tie through both of the holes and fasten it. It'll be much harder for homeless people (or anyone for that matter!) to remove your signs.

Make sure you bring a map with you and mark down all of the locations that you have your signs. You will need to go back about once a month to make sure they are still there, and that's a lot easier when you know where they were!

Apps

Gathering Knowledge and Asking Questions

The first stop on the list is always Facebook. Facebook is a great place to find groups of people who are doing exactly what you are doing. I'm growing a Facebook group full of investors trying to improve their investing skills, so if you want to connect with me and other like-minded individuals, please go www.MateosMobiles.com/FB. But don't just stop at my group! Go find other Facebook groups as well by searching for "Mobile Home Investors". They say you shouldn't advertise for your competitors, but I want everyone to read this book to get as much help as possible.

Another great place to ask questions is BiggerPockets.com. You can ask all of your questions there as well. Sometimes people even answer them! BiggerPockets is also a great place to look for buyers. If you post that you are a mobile home wholesaler, then you will more than likely get a couple of calls.

Finding Leads

Facebook Marketplace is my first stop when searching for mobile homes for sale. I set my radius to as far as I'm willing to drive. I try to browse through what people have to offer at least once a day, usually with my morning coffee! Just make sure you filter the search to "Mobile Homes" or else, you might end up buying a new set of chairs and a coffee bar like I did last month!

Once I've looked at leads on Facebook, I head over to my second favorite website - Craigslist. You can use Craigslist in two ways, by either searching for buyers/sellers OR by looking through the buyer/seller listings.

You will often find people posting "We buy mobile homes!" ads on Craigslist as well as people advertising mobile homes. Call the "We buy mobile homes!" adds because that is exactly how you get hooked up with wholesalers. You should also call, text, or email all mobile home sellers to try to set up an appointment with them. Do not talk price, just set up a showing!

If you'd prefer people call you, you can put an ad up on Craigslist. It used to be free but they made it $5 to put in any real estate ad just recently. You'll need to refresh it each week to stay relevant. It should include a few pictures and some short ad copy. For example.

> We buy mobile homes | Fast | Cash | As-is
>
>
>
> Are you trying to sell your mobile home? We can help!
> Call or email us for more information at ….

An even more clever way to use listings is to look at the rentals available. Not many real estate investors will look here and you can use this to your advantage. Some of these landlords might be on the fence about being a landlord for another year and just need a little push or "sign from god" to get them to sell. The flip side is that most of the calls you make will be duds. Remember that real estate is a numbers game. Keep at it and you'll unearth a good lead now and then before it hits the market.

Every now and then you'll find an investor who doesn't want to sell but really wants to outsource the management of their portfolio to someone else. Many real estate investors get their start by master leasing such properties.

A master lease is a contract where you agree to manage properties for a landlord by subletting them. You'll pay the landlord a monthly sum that is slightly below market value. You'll then manage those properties by either sprucing them up to attract better tenants or simply advertise those properties for rents that are towards the higher side and earn a profit. You'll have what is called an equitable title on the property. This lets you make modifications and renovate it to generate higher rents.

Master leasing a group of homes in a mobile home park is a great way to get started if you don't have the cash to invest in your own yet. If you run into this opportunity and are interested in being a landlord yourself then make sure you take it! Within a year not only will you have enough money to invest in your own mobile home, you'll also have experience *on another investor's dime.* Always be on the lookout for new investing opportunities. You never know where your next lead will come from.

Other apps and websites you can use are Kijiji (specifically if you're in Canada), 5miles, and listing sites such as Zillow and Redfin.

Park Managers

If you're looking for mobile homes, why not go right to the source? Visit the mobile home parks and get to know the managers, who may or may not be the owner of the park.

The manager is usually up to speed with how things work in the park and will be able to tell you how much rent is, what the tenant are like, and which lots are coming up for sale or have issues with them. Of course, you may need to ask them a few questions before you get all of this information. The park managers are used to being ignored by most people who come in and are usually cordial but do not give you detailed answers.

It might sound strange, but treating them like people and trying to connect with them on a human level will make them more likely to help you. There are a few strategies that you can use to do just that, all of which take a varying amount of time.

Making Friends

All those life coaches aren't lying when they say first impressions are important. Make sure you are dressed and act professionally. If they look busy, then ask them short and to the point questions. If they don't, then try to get them chit-chatting. You can talk about the park at first, but also try to ask them some simple personal questions as well (but not too personal!). Everyone likes talking about themselves. Try to find something they like talking about and ask them all about it. For instance, if they like talking about their kids, ask them a few questions about their kids. If they are in a local soccer league, ask them what position they play, how long they've played, etc. Make sure you also get the information about the park that you need as well! Don't allow yourself to walk away with a lot of new knowledge about soccer but no new information about the park!

Once you've made a great first impression, you can move on to Phase 2. This basically involves reminding the park manager that you exist. Call them about once a month and ask if there are any mobile homes for sale. You can also try to chit chat if you have the time for it and they don't seem too busy. But fair warning: Don't make every conversation you have with them a long one because people will avoid calling you if they know you're going to waste their time.

You should also send them cards for major holidays. Christmas, and 4th of July are my go-tos because they're just about six months apart. Address the card to the park manager (or managers if you talk to more than one) and send it to the mobile home park's clubhouse address. They'll get a kick out of it! I automate mine with this service: https://www.postable.com.

Free Mobile Homes!

Make sure these park managers know that you are interested in any mobile homes that are for sale or need to be removed from the park. Let them know that you'll move them for free as long as you get to keep the home. Sometimes, people abandon their old homes and leave it up to the park to move it. This a great opportunity for you to come in and remove it free of charge, as long as you get to keep the home! Once you have it, you can wholesale it, flip it, or simply move it to another park and rent it out. All you have to do is pay the moving fees.

Mobile Homes for Sale

Some parks are owned by big corporations that try to keep their community looking well maintained and fresh. These corporations routinely replace old homes because it keeps their park modern and allows them to charge more rent. Normally, they try to sell or even throw away the old homes. They're landlords, not flippers!

Fortunately, you are. Find these big players and get to know the park manager. It might sound far-fetched to you, but every once in a while you'll land 10 units at $1,000 a pop or even less.

If you want to wholesale them, all you have to do is find an end buyer who is willing to move the mobile home and pay you more than what you paid for it!

If you want to flip it, you'll need to include the moving costs and repair costs in your flip estimate and find a place to temporarily put the mobile home. Sometimes, you can buy a lot in another park but if you're trying to professionally flip mobile homes, it is worth it to have an acre or two of land in a rural area near where you live. That way, you have a place you can dump these mobile homes while you fix them. The holding cost of land is usually very cheap and once you've flipped it, you can ask the buyer to pay to move it. You can also turn your flips into a mobile home park and sell the park after you've filled it for even more than you would get for each individual flip.

If the mobile homes aren't in too bad of shape (they just need a coat of paint and some minor repairs), all you need to do is find another park that has some open plots and rent it out as is. Put them back on the market for rent and you'll earn massive cash flow every month. What's more, if you approach a park manager with a portfolio of 10 homes that you'd like to place on their property, you might even score a lot fee discount which further boosts your cash flow.

Tax Sales

This particular tactic doesn't always work for mobile homes but attending tax sales is a great way to pick up some decent properties. A tax sale can either be a foreclosure sale or a tax lien sale.

What's the difference?

In a foreclosure, the entire property is being sold. Perhaps the owner cannot afford to make payments on it anymore and the bank is looking to sell it at an auction.

A lien sale is a different beast altogether.

Counties and local governments collect property taxes to fund their municipal departments (police, fire departments, etc.) If a homeowner falls behind on their property taxes, a lien is placed on the property. Here's the thing about tax liens. They're the first lien on a property no matter what. They come ahead of mortgages as well. If a bank owns the mortgage lien on the property and you own the tax lien, you get first dibs on the property if the borrower defaults on their mortgage payments[7].

Mobile homes usually don't have property tax lien issues but you never know when one might crop up. The local government advertises tax lien auctions and foreclosures on their website. These auctions have specific rules and codes of conduct so make sure you read up on these topics before attending one. Different states have different bidding systems and auction processes. However, most of these sales require cash the day you buy the mobile home so make sure you have an investment partner with cash or are ready to throw some of your own cash in the ring.

You should also look up the addresses of these properties beforehand and at least send someone from WeGoLook.com or Facebook Marketplace to take pictures of all four sides of the properties. If you can go yourself, that's even better! If you have the time to go look at these properties, make sure you look at the exteriors and take note of any damage!

If the home doesn't have a skirt, that likely means the underbelly has been destroyed from weather damage. If the roof tiles are falling off, you can assume leaks. If the gutters look like they're being held on by a hope and a prayer, it's probably not a good sign for the interior.

You should try to get a peek at the inside if you can. Sometimes the blinds, windows, or even doors are open. Never enter the property because that is trespassing, but make sure you have a pretty good idea if the property is going to be a bad investment before you buy it in a tax lien sale. I don't suggest you do this, but some investors pretend to be salesmen in order to knock on the door and get a look at the inside. Remember to follow all your local laws!

When you go to these sales, it's very easy to get caught up in the excitement of bidding. Just remember, it's better to let a good deal that looks fishy go than to take a chance and get a bad deal!

Mobile Home Dealerships

Mobile Home Dealerships are another great place to find free mobile homes. It might sound kind of backwards because a mobile home dealership is usually the place you go to buy a mobile home, but what a lot of beginners don't realize is that for almost every home they sell, they have to move an old one.

Seems like they would just sell those old ones at the dealership, right? Well, oftentimes, the price of moving the mobile home, storing it in their lot (instead of a brand new one!) and waiting to sell it is more expensive than simply paying a shipping company to throw these old units away. But, you, as a mobile home investor, can help!

Go into these dealerships and ask to speak with the sales manager. Let them know that you will remove any mobile home from any lot for free - as long as you get to keep it. Just like when you offered to do this for the park managers, that free mobile home will be yours for just the price of shipping. All you need to do once you land a "free" home is go online and look for mobile home transportation companies.

You should try to follow up with these sales managers as much as you follow up with the mark managers! Call or visit them about once a month and send them a Christmas and 4th of July card! (For our non-American readers, find 2-3 holidays that are popular in your country and send a card or your country's equivalent for those.)

If you find that a particular mobile home is too ratty to fix up, or that you just want to wholesale them, look for transportation companies that have their own park or have a relationship with a park, then just wholesale it to them for $3000-$5000. Tell them they can have it for that price as long as they move it!

Negotiation

Once you've put all of the above methods into action, you're going to start receiving leads. Most of them will be duds but you'll find a good lead here and there. Be consistent with your lead generation efforts. Don't slack when the times are good. You need to market whether times are good or bad. It's a numbers game at the end of the day. The more marketing you do, the more money you'll make. Eventually, you will find out what your success rates are and tailor your ad spend to what works.

For instance, maybe you'll discover you get one call per month for every bandit sign you put out. Or maybe you'll find that you have to drive through five mobile home parks to find one home worth purchasing. As you do this more and get better at it, you'll figure out exactly how much time you need to make one full deal.

Once you get strong leads on board you will need to negotiate with them. You want to try to find motivated sellers who are ready to offload their properties. The thing is, these motivated sellers might not be that motivated the first time you talk to them… or the second… or the third.

Real estate is a numbers game. I know I've said that three times so far, but it's true. Not only do you need to talk with a lot of people, you need to follow up with all of these people after you speak with them! Every no has the potential to turn into a yes!

Maybe your seller isn't exactly motivated but is sitting on the fence between being convinced to sell and holding on to their mobile home. I like to call these fence-sitters future motivated sellers. My job is to help them convince themselves that they want to get rid of their mobile home - quickly and easily!

You will come across a lot of future motivated sellers. As you get more experience speaking with them, you'll learn that there are really two steps in turning them into true motivated sellers: building rapport and figuring out their why. Let's dive into this, shall we?

Building Rapport

Just like I explained earlier with advertising, people are far more likely to work with you if they trust you and like you, so you need to make sure you come off as trustworthy and likeable. One way to do this is to spend some time with them. If you are funny, try to make them laugh. If you find that you have a shared interest, talk about that interest and maybe share some books or Youtube videos that you liked.

Even after you build some rapport, they still might not sell to you. Sometimes, the deal doesn't work for them that day, but circumstances can and do change! A no today might turn into a yes tomorrow. Remember to grab their phone number and ask if you can text them later on. Then, in about a month, ask how their mobile home sale went. If they haven't sold it yet, this might be the trigger to them selling it to you because they know they'll get rid of it immediately.

Finding Out their Why

The other thing you must do when you speak with these sellers is to figure out why they are selling their mobile home. Every seller usually has one or two reasons why they are selling it and a plan in their head about how and when it will be sold. Most of the time, you just need to ask the right questions to figure out their why.

For instance, if they're trying to sell their mobile home before their rent is up because they're going to move to another state, then you know there are several reasons they want to sell their home. First, they need to move, so they have a deadline. Second, they might need money to move all of their stuff away, so they have a certain bottom of the barrel number in mind for how much they are willing to sell their mobile home for.

If I were in that situation, I'd follow up by asking if they were planning on using the money from the mobile home to finance their move. If the answer is yes, then I would ask how much they thought they needed. Sometimes, these sellers have thought about how much they'll need and other times they haven't. Whatever number they throw out, that's usually the bare minimum that they are willing to accept. From there, you have a few options. You can either offer them a flat amount right above that or you can offer that amount as a down payment and ask if they'd be willing to seller-finance the rest. It all depends on your budget and strategy.

Another common reason is they are upgrading to a stick-built home. This is an extremely exciting time in someone's life but it is also very stressful. The pain point in this case is that they have to pay lot fees on top of their new mortgage until they can sell their old mobile home. They also probably want to make a little bit of money from the sale so they can add it to their down payment or use it to buy furniture.

"Ah, so you want to sell it because every month it sits here, you're paying $400 in lot fees and taxes, right?"

The above is a very simple sentence that reminds these people what they are missing out on if they don't sell. They're missing out on a minimum of $400 bucks a month!

"How long have you been trying to sell this?"

Is another one of my favorites. If it's been more than 3 months, then no doubt you have someone who is very willing to negotiate.

I hope you see the pattern here. You just need to figure out why it is they are moving and what they were hoping to pay for with the money from the sale. Once you have that information, weave it into the conversation. Subtly remind them of the downside to holding out for a better deal while highlighting all the upsides of them selling their mobile home *to you now.*

Adopt the Right Approach

The best approach to adopt in a negotiation is win-win. This means both you and the seller get to benefit. This is in direct opposition to the popular method of negotiation, which is to try to bully the other side into giving you what you want. You don't want to be known as a bully because word will get out and people will not want to sell anything to you. You want to be known as an investor who is kind and fair but firm.

Offering a Price

Go through the checklist at www.MateosMobiles.com/mobiles and mark off anything you think is wrong with the property. Let the buyer know you'll buy it as-is. Every old property has quirks and mobile homes are no exception. You should let the seller know that you will buy the property on their schedule and pay cash. You can also throw in a few goodies like paying the seller's moving fees.

Do not go above a price that you are comfortable with. Remember, this is a win-win scenario, so you are expecting yourself to win as well.

Walk Away

Most of the sellers you'll encounter won't necessarily need to sell, so they likely won't sell at a price that will work for your profit margins, and that's ok! We aren't in the business of ripping people off, we're in the business of helping people that really need to get rid of their property.

Don't ever be so desperate to buy a property that you cannot walk away from it. It's best to adopt an air of calm detachment with any deal. If purchasing that mobile home doesn't make financial sense to you, let the seller know and walk away.

Some sellers are playing hardball when you are negotiating but are actually very motivated to sell. These hardball motivated sellers will "change their mind" and try to sell you their mobile home at the price you wanted. This doesn't happen all the time but if you stay focused and make good business decisions it will happen sometimes.

A Note on Rentals

If you are purchasing a property for the specific purpose of renting it then I am of the firm belief that you do not have to squeeze every penny out of your seller. You can probably find a pretty decent property for around $20,000, figure out what they want as a down payment, and then draft up a seller finance deal for the rest. This is just one man's opinion, but you don't need to try to find an extremely motivated seller if you're just trying to buy a rental. You just need to find a mobile home in decent shape that is being sold for a price that you think you can pay off within two years.

4

STEP 2: THE EXPERIENCED INVESTOR'S SECRET TO DUE DILIGENCE AND WALKTHROUGHS

Finding a mobile home is just the first part of actually making money with them. The next step in the process is to determine if they'll be profitable. Before you've put the mobile home under contract, you need to go physically look at it, inspect it yourself, and run the numbers.

After a lot of research and trial and error, I've created a checklist that will help you find most issues with any mobile home. You can download this checklist from www.MateosMobiles.com/mobiles. Print it out and make sure you bring it to every mobile home you visit. Not only will it help you determine if you should purchase that property, it will also give a visual to the seller of what work needs to be done. This can help you with negotiation.

This chapter is an apt companion to that checklist because it focuses on what to look for when you try to buy a mobile home and how to tell if it was used or if it was loved because there is a difference! Mobile homes are simple but they do require you to keep up with their maintenance schedule so you can catch problems early and fix them before they become catastrophes. If you, or any mobile home owner for that matter, don't lovingly keep up with the maintenance schedule, it will cause very obvious problems that will need to be fixed.

I'll give you a list of issues to look out for and try to give you an estimate on exactly how much it might cost to fix each one. Of course, contractor and material prices are very regional so I will be talking in very broad terms.

The state of disrepair you are willing to accept completely depends on what you are trying to do with mobile homes. If you're just trying to buy a few to rent them out, you probably want to buy homes that have been taken care of, at least until you get yourself acquainted with the process of them renting out. If you're looking to flip them, then obviously you'll be looking to find abused mobile homes because those are the most profitable. Wholesalers should be open to homes of any condition.

This chapter is going to give you the lowdown on which problems can be fixed and which you ought to stay away from.

Common Issues With Mobile Homes

Let me start off by saying that any mobile home that was manufactured before 1985 is scrap. There are two reasons for this: First, 1985 is now 35 years ago, which is just about how long the manufacturers expected those homes to last anyway. After 1985, they are expected to last around 55 years. Keep that in mind as you're looking at mobile homes!

Second, the housing code was restructured after 1985. Every home built before this isn't to spec and is not going to give your tenants a good living experience. If you see any home for sale that was manufactured before this, use extreme caution. It might literally fall apart if you try to move it.

With that out of the way, let's move on and take a look at some of the most common problems that afflict mobile homes. This isn't an exhaustive list but it covers most issues that you will commonly see.

Foundations

Mobile homes typically use a pier and tie down system to help them maintain a solid foundation. The ground under the home should slope down away from the center. This will ensure water doesn't collect under the home and weaken the foundation.

Piers can be made of steel or cinder blocks and the frame is tied to the ground using steel straps. Problems arise when the piers don't rest on a stable cement foundation. If they rest directly on the ground this causes the floor of the home to eventually sag.

Walk around the home and check if there are any areas where the floor sags. If so, get under the home and see what the foundation looks like. Check for rust and any other forms of decay. Piers that are bent or aren't vertical can be replaced, along with the foundation. Most of these jobs will cost a maximum of $3,000.

Windows and Door Frames

A poor foundation places stress on the structure and causes doors and windows to fall out of alignment. Open and close every door to check how it fits into its frame. Check to see if the windows behave properly as well.

This is usually a relatively minor problem that can be fixed by adjusting the hinges or asking a handyman to use wood shims to adjust the way the door or window fits into its frame. This is a pretty cheap fix and can probably be done in an hour or two for a few hundred bucks.

In a rare case, this issue can be caused by a sagging foundation so if you found problems with the foundation earlier, that is likely the cause of the misalignment. Once you have the foundation fixed, these windows and doors will more than likely need their hinges adjusted because they are probably bent.

Roofs

Roofs are always an issue with homes and mobile homes are no different. Mobile homes have different types of roofs. Older homes will have an asphalt shingle roof. Over time the shingles dry out and curl around the edges. This results in water leaks. Replacing these types of roofs will cost you between $4,000 to $6,000. Another older model of roof is the rolled steel version.

These roofs have steel sheets welded together to form one continuous roofing structure. Over time, the sheets can rust and the seams between the sheets can become weak. Take a look at the state of the roof and, if you can get up there, try to walk on it - but be careful!

If you notice water or moisture congregating around the seams, this is a sign of trouble. You can seal leaks with a sealant that will cost you a few hundred dollars. If the roof is very damaged, you can either replace it or put a rubber roof over it. This will usually cost you around $3,000.

Water Leaks

Homes are made of wood and if leaks aren't addressed quickly, the entire structure will rot. Rotting structures is actually the number one problem I see with mobile homes! Water gets into the wood and just destroys it.

While most people focus on roof leaks, window and door leaks can be even more damaging because the floors and exterior walls are the actual structure of the home itself! There aren't any steel beams in there. Damage or rot to these structures could result in the entire home needing extensive rehabbing. Have you heard of tearing it down to the studs? That would be what you'd have to do in this case. Tear it down to the studs of the home, cut out the rotted wood. Put in new wood, then rebuild the walls and floors. Yikes!

Window leaks are far worse to deal with than floor leaks because replacing a wall is much more expensive than replacing a section of the floor. Make sure you push against every wall in the house to see if it "gives." If you can see any rot on the surface, this is a bad sign. It means the rot is far worse inside the wall.

If you come across a mobile home with this kind of damage, you have a few options. I would seriously ask you to think hard about how much work you'd like to put into flipping this mobile home. Structural damage is one of the few red flags in mobile homes that should give you pause because it is rather expensive to fix.

If you're deadset on making money from this home, then hiring 2-3 contractors to come give you a bid is an absolute must. You need a few of them because you don't want to be tricked by an unscrupulous contractor. If the bids and timeframes are about the same, you at least know that you're on the right track. Make sure you follow my advice and use ThumbTack.com to find an honest contractor.

You could also try to wholesale this home. I do not think you'll get very much money for it because it does need some very extensive work. If you find another investor who likes to flip mobile homes, you could offer to split the profits with them 50/50 and enter into a one-time partnership. This would be great for you because it will give you a free mentor!

Ceilings

Ceilings are purely cosmetic.

If you didn't have a ceiling, you'd see the trusses and the roof. The roof is what catches all of the rain, snow, and other things that fall out of the sky. So, if the ceiling needs work, then it's usually a cheap fix.

Older homes contain acoustical tiles or drywall for ceilings. Ceiling damage is mostly caused due to unaddressed roof leaks. The best way to detect cosmetic ceiling issues is to look for discoloration at the edges of where the ceiling tiles meet the wall. Look for loose or bubbling paint on the ceiling drywall.

If you only see this discoloration or bubbling then the problem is likely cosmetic. That means you just need to replace sections of the ceiling. This is a quick, easy, and cheap repair that you could probably handle yourself if you wanted to! (If you find that acoustical panels are damaged, consider replacing them with drywall. It's cheap and a lot easier to deal with.)

However, if you see sections of the ceiling warping and rotting, there are likely structural issues with the trusses. This brings us back into the world of structural damage and will require the ThumbTack.com general contractors to come out and give you an estimate.

You can replace and repair sections of the trusses but it will be expensive. You'll also likely need to replace the cosmetic material entirely. The good news is, if the trusses are damaged, you can use this to seriously negotiate the price down with your seller, because it will be very expensive to fix and the price will vary based on how much damage there is.

Plumbing and Wiring

Plumbing is one area where mobile homes shine. It's pretty easy to repair most pipes because they are exposed under the foundation.

This makes it easy to tell if your home has PB or PolyButylene pipes! That's great news because if you find the home has these pipes, you can use it to negotiate about $1000 of your purchase price because they will need to be replaced.

Older mobile homes will probably have PB pipes. PB was once pushed as the future of plumbing thanks to its low cost. However, everyone soon found out that chlorine and other chemicals in the water supply caused the pipes to rot from the inside out.

PB usage is a serious issue. You might find that your insurance premiums are extremely high or you might even be denied coverage. If you find pipes that have been stamped with a "PB2110" sign, replace them!

Most mobile homes don't have wiring issues... with the notable exception of mobile homes that had an amateur wiring job added on by their previous owner. Many owners add wings to their homes and just add their new wires to the old system. This can cause load issues with a box that hasn't been designed to absorb the additional capacity.

If there are no additions or if the additions were done professionally, you can probably get away with not having an electrician look at the box. If not, it might be worth it to have an electrician, inspector or general contractor look at the box to see if there are any issues.

Owner Additions

Owner additions are pretty common and are usually pretty poorly done. HUD specifies that the frame and outer walls should be able to carry their own weight. If you find any structure is adding weight to the existing mobile home's original outer walls then this is in violation of HUD rules. Porches and covered awnings are the most common additions you'll find. If awnings are made of aluminum and have been professionally installed, then it probably isn't too much of an issue. However, if you believe that an amateur built it, you'll probably have to have a contractor fix it or remove it.

If an add-on structure larger than an awning exists, look at how it transfers its weight. These structures need to transfer it to the ground and avoid relying on the existing frame for support. If that system isn't in place, consider tearing the additional structure down or installing proper load-bearing systems to handle the weight.

Heating and Cooling

Like most people, mobile home owners usually want their homes to be cool in the summer and warm in the winter. HVAC (Heating Ventilation Air Conditioning) issues may cause problems with this and the repair costs vary depending on the level of damage the system has sustained. A telltale sign is the presence of additional window AC units or heaters in a home. This means the central ventilation system isn't working well.

The furnace and air handler in a mobile home are typically built into a closet and feed air down to the central ducts underneath the home. The units within the closet might not be working well and might need to be replaced. These are straightforward to fix and you can buy them at any big box or scratch and dent store (my personal favorite!). However, issues with the ducts such as leaks or rust will give you a harder time.

Duct issues will require you to replace the entire ducting system. Check the ducts to see if there's any debris present and confirm none of the ducts are bent or damaged. If you don't need to replace the ducts, consider removing the unit from within the closet and installing an external HVAC handler. You can buy a used or refurbished one for under $2,000. This will increase the closet space within the home and you can charge more rent on that basis.

Insulation

In mobile homes, insulation exists in the attic, outer walls, and under the floor. The insulation under the floor is held in place by a heavy gauge plastic sheet. These often become punctured and fall out, especially during plumbing repairs when holes need to be cut into the sheeting. These holes are often never resealed or they're sealed improperly. Over time, the hole reappears and this causes a whole host of issues.

One major issue is that pests use these holes to get in the mobile home. Sometimes, water can collect within the insulation which can cause mold, water damage, and ultimately a saggy floor.

The only solution to this problem is to replace it with a new plastic sheet and screw it to the floor joists. Make sure you have a contractor or a handyman quote you on what this type of repair will cost if you see it because they can be more expensive than you think!

Washer Drains

A huge problem with poorly maintained mobile homes is the washer draining directly to the ground instead of into the main sewer drain. This is a huge problem since water collecting underneath the home will result in mold and can even cause the foundation to develop serious problems. If you find washer pipes draining like this make sure they're extended to connect directly to the sewer pipe.

The same issue applies to dryer vents venting directly into the crawl space. If you see this, you can bet there will be mold problems under the floor. Lint also collects in these areas which poses a fire hazard. The dryer venting needs to be run through the skirting to the outside.

Skirting

Skirting is extremely important, in it is second only to the roof in terms of safety structures. They can be made of cement block, wood, aluminum, or fiberglass. Damaged skirting can cause pest infestation and moisture damage in the crawl space. Repair it quickly to make sure no damage occurs. If there is no skirt, then you should be really careful. Ask the owner how long there hasn't been a skirt around the home. If it's been more than a few months, negotiate a much lower price because missing skirts can cause a lot of very expensive foundation and plumbing problems.

Fixing and Flipping

Some of these repairs are more expensive than others, but making any repair is fine as long as you account for it in your budget. It's very important to estimate repairs before you make your offer because this can really affect your bottom line. Especially if you underestimate it!

Using an Inspector

Underestimating repair costs is a major issue that many new investors have. Creating a bid is one way that you can avoid over- or under-estimating repair costs.

To create a bid, you will either need to create an itemized list of what you believe is wrong with the unit (which your inspector will provide) or you will need to ask a contractor to perform a walkthrough and create an itemized list themself.

If your seller doesn't want contractors walking through their mobile home, then you'll probably have to pay an inspector.

Make sure the inspector takes detailed photos of anything he finds. This will help the contractors determine exactly how much they will need to spend if they do not get to look at the house. Alternatively, you could terminate the deal if the owner does not let you set up a time for contractors to perform a walkthrough. The choice is yours, though I would err on the side of working with the owner to get the deal done. Remember, you're creating a win-win scenario so as long as they allow an inspector, you should try to work with them.

Contractors

If your seller only allowed an inspector to walk through the home, then you have to wait for him to create an itemized list so you can give that to your prospective contractors. You should organize the repair list into 3-5 draws (planned payments to contractors).

What that means is you should split the work up into 3-5 parts by grouping like jobs together and ordering them in a way that makes sense to the workflow (don't worry - the contractors will let you know if the order you select doesn't make sense. Generally, just keep sections of things together). You only pay your contractor when they complete a draw.

As I've said before, there are a lot of very honest people in this business but there are some dishonest ones as well. Most contractors expect you to structure your contract in this way so don't be afraid to drop the ones that complain. They're usually the ones you should stay away from anyway.

Let's say you have a mobile home that needs the roof repaired and the plumbing repaired. You also want to upgrade the kitchen and repaint. You'd split this up into an itemized list that is categorized by the main structure. In a very simple contract, that looks like the following:

1. Roof
2. Plumbing
3. Kitchen Upgrade
4. Paint

Then, you'd only pay your contractor after they complete a job. If they need an initial infusion of money for roof materials, you can agree to give them that but you'd only pay for labor after the roof is completed. Make sure you draw up a contract stating that you will not owe them anything until all the repairs in that bid have been made (I like using rocketlawyer.com for this type of contract) and get cracking!

Handymen

A handyman is different than a general contractor. Handymen are usually skilled laborers who know how to do odd jobs like fix drywall, paint, and patch roofs. I want to make the distinction between general contractors and handymen here because some jobs are simple and just need a handyman while other jobs are complicated and need a general contractor who has the appropriate licensing to legally complete it.

Since handymen usually work for themselves and don't have licenses, they are generally much cheaper than general contractors who do need licensing and often outsource a lot of the work to their team.

With that out of the way, let's talk about some minor issues that you can probably fix with a limited budget.

Roof Leaks

If you find that the roof is compromised, try to replace portions of it instead of the entire roof. Sometimes this isn't possible. If the roof is too badly damaged, no amount of patches will be able to salvage it.

To determine if a patch will work, all you need to do is find out where the leaks are. If there are only a few then you can probably patch it. If you see multiple leakage issues in the roof, then you will likely need to replace the entire roof.

If the roof of your mobile home needs to be replaced, first determine what kind of a roof it is. Asphalt shingle roofs will cost you $650 - $2,500 to replace for single-wide homes. You can double those costs for a double-wide. If the roof is rolled steel, you're going to have to spend more. This is because you'll have to either put a roof over the steel roof or you'll have to install a rubber roof.

"Roofing over" involves installing an asphalt shingle on top of the steel roof. This will cost between $1,000 to $2,000 for a single-wide. Rubber roofs cost around the same. These roofs are sheets that are stretched over the steel roof and act like a membrane to prevent damage. The costs I've mentioned are just the material costs. You'll have to pay labor costs as well, which will run you anywhere from $500 to $3,000 for a single-wide.

Floor Issues

Soft spots on the floor can be replaced easily. As I mentioned in the previous section, wall damage caused by window leaks are far more troublesome and expensive to fix. Soft spots on floors can be fixed by removing the rotten plywood and replacing it with fresh wood of equal thickness. This isn't very expensive and is only a few hours of work. If you're really short on cash, you can do it yourself after watching a few Youtube videos.

Walls

There are two sides to a wall in a mobile home: exterior and interior. There are also different types of walls to deal with. On the exterior, you'll find either aluminum, wood, vinyl, or cement fiberboard. Let's look at them in turn.

Aluminum tends to get dented quite easily but the panels are also easy to replace. Each panel costs around $40 and can be installed within half an hour.

Wood siding gives the home a richer look but gets damaged much more easily. It costs around the same as aluminum.

Cement fiberboard is a new development and is probably the best of the lot. It rarely ever gets damaged or rots and the paint lasts longer than the other options. It is expensive to install but well worth it because it will probably outlast the mobile home!

Vinyl siding is the most attractive option but it doesn't come cheap. It's quite durable, as durable as cement fiberboard, but is far more expensive. You can expect to spend upwards of $5,000 or even $10,000 on installation and material costs.

Onto the interior!

If your walls are rotten, there's nothing you can do. No amount of money can fix it and it's very rare that substantial investment can save such a home from being scrapped. However, if you just see some holes (like someone punched the wall or maybe the corner of some furniture made a hole) you can easily fix them. This can be as simple as patching the drywall with new drywall or replacing old panels with new ones. Replace these tiny holes and you'll immediately increase the resale value.

Alternatively, if the mobile home looks outdated because it looks like a museum dedicated to the 90's, you can repaint, retile, and remove walls to add a lot of value.

2010 saw the rise of open-concept homes like never before and this trend was definitely found in mobile homes as well. The great thing about mobile home interior walls is that they aren't load bearing so you can remove as many as you want.

Older mobile homes will come with interior wood paneling. Thankfully, upgrading the look of these old homes is fairly straightforward. All you have to do is caulk the seams and paint over the wood paneling. You'll need an oil based primer to get the paint to stick to the wall which can cost you around $1,500 for the entire interior. If you choose to do this and don't have experience painting, this type of job can easily be done by a ThumbTack handyman or professional painter.

Plumbing

If you find the leak is coming from a pipe that is exposed in the crawlspace, you might be able to fix it on your own. However, I highly recommend asking a professional to do all plumbing work. Luckily, mobile homes don't usually have a lot of plumbing issues unless the skirt has been removed for a long period of time.

Wiring Issues

The first thing to do is to check whether everything works. Sometimes, the seller might shut the power off which prevents you from evaluating the state of the wiring. Insist on it being turned back on so that you can inspect it. Also, have your inspector check the outlets with a multimeter. A reading between 110-120 volts means everything's good.

The good news is that you generally won't have to deal with too many wiring or electrical issues and fortunately, they likely won't be very expensive to fix (around $500), with the exception being if the electrician needs to make holes in the drywall. Then, the wiring issue might not be that expensive but the drywall holes sure will! If you don't want to try to patch them yourself, then a ThumbTack handyman should do the trick.

Appliances and HVAC

Mobile homes will typically come with a stove and a fridge. Make sure these appliances are in working order when you inspect the property. If the seller has switched the power off, have them turn it back on. If this is not possible for some reason and if you can't inspect these appliances before you buy the property, you should assume they're broken and be pleasantly surprised if they are not...

You don't have to provide new appliances to your tenants but whatever appliances you make available in the home should be in good working order. There's no need to provide washing machines or dryers with the property.

However, you should test the HVAC systems thoroughly and look for the defects I outlined earlier. If the HVAC is broken, it will definitely need to be repaired by a professional.

Clean

The easiest way to spruce up a property is to thoroughly clean it. Here are some things to look out for when you're trying to clean a property.

1. **Bad smells**. These can often be addressed with a new round of paint and a good carpet cleaning.
2. **Dust**. Pay attention to the baseboards and other small crevices where people don't normally look. A little bit of dust can go a long way towards giving the mobile home an air of uncleanliness.
3. **Signs of infestations**. Pay close attention to the spaces in which the walls, ceilings and floors meet.
4. **Mold**. You will need to look both in the mobile home and under it. Push on the walls, walk all over the floors, and inspect the bathrooms thoroughly for mold of any kind.

5. **Furniture or junk**. This should all be removed.
6. **Pressure wash the exterior of the home**. The outside is the first thing someone sees. Pressure washers are not very expensive to rent and even more cost efficient to purchase.
7. **Give it a fresh coat of paint**. While this isn't necessary, it can be done fairly cheaply by a handyman if pressure washing didn't do the trick. If the interior looks sad or you had to cover drywall holes, then you'll likely need to paint it as well.
8. **Carpet**. I already mentioned this in the first section about bad smells, but hiring a carpet cleaner can greatly restore disgusting carpet. If the carpet looks tired, you can hire a carpet steaming company to come out and deep clean it. This probably won't cost you more than a couple hundred bucks and could seriously improve the look and smell of the mobile home. (If the carpet is still extremely ratty and stained after this, then you might consider replacing it.) If you're going to rent out this mobile home, there isn't really a reason to put fresh carpet in there as your renters will probably just mess it up anyway. If you're trying rehab the mobile home, then putting fresh carpet in might be worth the expense, however I find that a deep clean usually works just fine, and you can do it yourself!

In my experience, a clean looking home with a few imperfections can sell for more than a dirty one without defects!

Windows

Windows used in a mobile home are usually standard sized. Older homes will have pretty dismal looking windows made of aluminum. It's a good idea to replace them to give your property a nice visual appeal. Another advantage of replacing the windows is that you'll boost the energy efficiency of your property massively.

You can opt for double-pane aluminum or vinyl to boost the appearance and energy efficiency. The top of the line is double-pane vinyl low E. Double-pane vinyl typically works best. You can expect to pay between $200 to $250 per window. This is a pretty low priority item that doesn't need to be done if it's going to affect your bottom line.

Increasing Curb Appeal

Once you're done inspecting it for the catastrophic problems, try to think through where you can improve the cosmetics. The most obvious improvements you can make are to the exterior, doors, and windows. Painting kitchen cabinets and putting down new vinyl floors are also great ways to cheaply increase the value of a home. I also like to install new bathroom fixtures that are modern looking but don't break the bank. These upgrades will add far more to the final price of the property than what they cost.

Painting or re-wallpapering is also a great way to increase a home's appeal. Retiling is also a good option to pursue. If you work with a handyman, they'll usually know the most up-to-date style and the cheapest materials you can buy.

There are two other areas where you can add value. The first is a shed. Mobile homes don't have as much space as a traditional home so sheds are invaluable. A small shed can cost you as little as $500 but the additional storage space can bring in thousands in value. The size of the shed you choose depends on the size of the home.

The second is an awning. In terms of quality of life, awnings are a great investment. They keep the weather away from the mainframe and make the home more livable in the summer since the sun doesn't hit the windows directly. If you plan on living in a home, installing an awning is worth it.

However, if you're planning on renting or reselling it, it's doubtful whether you'll recover your investment. This is because awnings cost a lot of money - $7,000 on average, and while they increase standard of living, they don't add that much value to the property.

Try to avoid the two mistakes new investors make - "fixing too much" and "fixing too little". If you fix too much, it leads to an increase in budget for no real added value. If you fix too little, it could give your business a bad name because you're just covering up all of the issues you find in a mobile home and ripping people off by selling polished junk.

Consider each repair or cosmetic upgrade carefully before you decide what to do. Obviously, you need to repair the mobile home so that it is livable, but you don't necessarily have to go above and beyond by repairing it with the most expensive options.

Similarly, before you upgrade any of the cosmetic items, make sure the upgrades you pick are popular in your area. If your area is fine with using subway tile on the kitchen counter, then do that! If no one else repainted their exterior, then maybe just a pressure wash will do. You can look at other homes in the neighborhood and other listings on Zillow to get a feel for what is normal for a flip in your area, and then all you have to do is copy it!

5

STEP 3: HOW TO DETERMINE WHAT THE MOBILE HOME IS WORTH AND NEGOTIATE A DISCOUNT

Now that you know what is wrong with your mobile home and you have a sense of what you're going to upgrade, you can add that calculation into your overall profit analysis. Before you purchase a mobile home, you need to know how much you're going to make from it so you can give an appropriate offer to the seller. This chapter intends to give you everything you need to do that.

There are a number of factors you need to consider when you are trying to figure out the value of any particular mobile home.

1. What's the price of other mobile homes in your area?
2. What shape is it in?
3. What brand is it?
4. How old is it?
5. Optics.

How Much Can I Sell them For

Selling anything comes down to two main questions: How does this compare to everything else in the area and what is everything else in the area selling theirs for.

Location

Since mobile homes are built to be transported, the location doesn't matter as much as more traditional real estate. There are quite a few mobile home aggregation websites and lists that you can post your deals on. If you want to try to sell your mobile home anywhere in your country, then you should look at some of these aggregation sites to get a feel for how much work is being done. It is a little more complicated but you can get more money this way if you're willing to be patient and possibly work out a deal with the buyer on the moving fees.

However, if you plan on keeping the mobile home where you found it, then you should treat your mobile home exactly like traditional real estate. If you have to flip it, you don't want to make it magnitudes nicer than the surrounding neighborhood.

Yes, you should fix your mobile home so that it is livable but you don't need to give it designer tiling if the rest of the mobile homes look like they are stuck in the 80's. Like SFRs, the other properties in your community have a very high impact on how much your mobile home will sell or rent for so you shouldn't break the bank if it's a mid or low tier neighborhood.

The rents will also be highly dependent on the location. Rent will obviously be higher if you're near a big city or a beautiful landscape.

Condition

A home that's in good condition will fetch more than one that is dilapidated. In fact, if the home doesn't come with the land, even a few dents and dings will send its market value crashing. This is good news for you as an investor since a few cheap upgrades and a little bit of sweat equity will restore a lot of its value.

And, as I said earlier, the condition of your home's exterior should be on par or maybe a little bit better than the mobile homes in that community.

That said, if the park is junky, it might be better to sell your home online to someone who wants it somewhere else and will buy it based only on your home's condition.

Make and Size of Home

Mobile Homes are a lot like cars. The make and model make a big difference in how much it is worth. You wouldn't pay the same price for a Honda as you would for a Ferrari, would you? There are a lot of different makes, but here's a quick cheat sheet for the most common:

Lower end: Fleetwood and Oakwood
Middle: Champions and Titans
High end: Palm Harbor Homes

So, when you are trying to figure out what a home will be worth, you need to take the make into consideration. Palm Harbor Homes will be worth more than Champion. And Champion homes will be worth more than Fleetwood.

If you're ever confused about the quality of your make, you can go onto the builder's website and look at what the new homes cost in comparison to other builders' homes. This should give you a pretty good idea whether you're buying a Honda or a Ferrari.

The size of the mobile home also plays an important role in the price. A single-wide will be almost half the price of the same double-wide version of that make. That said, single-wides and double-wides both have a range of square feet. So, it is still important to know exactly how much square feet your mobile home has for comparison. It is also good to take note of how many bedrooms, how many bathrooms, and if there are any additions. These can all affect the value as well.

Age

When it comes to mobile homes and age, you should think of them like you think of cars. The older the home is, the less it will be worth. However, an old, well-taken-care of mobile home can be worth more than a junky new one.

If it looks really bad on the inside, but it is structurally sound, you should probably buy it. Usually you can greatly increase the value by sprucing up the interior.

Optics

Your pictures and ad copy make a difference in what people believe the mobile home is worth. A few professionally taken pictures in a staged mobile home can go a long way toward increasing the perceived value. We'll talk more about that in the next chapter!

So How Much is it Worth?

Like all other real estate deals, you need to run "comps" on mobile homes in order to discover how much it is worth. A comp is when you find recently sold properties that are located in the same area and are similar to your prospective property. You take their sales price, find the average price per square foot, and use this to determine approximately what people will pay for your property.

If you are going to flip or wholesale, it is also important to understand the "after repair value" or ARV of a mobile home. The price people are willing to pay for a mobile home that needs work and a mobile home that was recently flipped are vastly different. That means when you comp this type of home, you will actually do it twice - once for the current, unflipped value and once for the ARV.

There are a few different ways that you can comp a mobile home that range from free to a few hundred dollars. No matter what real estate you invest in, I always recommend you comp it yourself.

However if you're new to comping, you should consider paying for an outside source to comp your first few deals as well. Comping is a skill and you will not be a perfect comper in the beginning. That's why you need to lean on a crutch because they will let you know if you are comping too high or too low. Don't worry, you won't be asking for their help forever. Eventually you will become a comping pro.

Comping a mobile home is just one step of your overall due diligence. If you've never done real estate before, due diligence is what you do to each deal before you buy it. Due diligence is all about checking everything you possibly can so that you have the most accurate read on your deal.

I like to split my due diligence into 2 parts: a cursory look and an in-depth look. When I find a mobile home, I do a 10 minute gut check to see if the deal makes sense. If it does, then I'll do a very in-depth look. This saves me hours of time each week because no matter how hard you try, some deals will never work.

Step 1. Cursory Comping

My gut check involves using free online tools to get a back of the napkin estimate on how much my deal might be worth before and after a flip. This takes me 5- 10 minutes per property. By the time it's complete, I have a picture of what I am willing to pay for the mobile home and what I am going to try to sell it for. At this point, you should already have a general idea of what needs to be repaired (from the description, pictures, and conversation with the owner) and loosely factor that in. You won't really know the repair estimate for sure until you physically (or virtually!) see the house.

Step 2. In-Depth Comping

If I determine that the investment makes sense, I make an appointment with the seller to go see it. Once there, I can determine what is actually wrong with the mobile home and update my repair estimates. Of course, if it needs more repairs then I will pay less to buy it.

If the in-depth comps tell me that I'll make a profit, I'll I extend an offer. Do not try to negotiate on the initial screening call, no matter what the seller tells you. Let them know that you can only make an accurate estimate after you see the home.

How to Comp

For the first step, aka gut check, my weapon of choice is Zillow. It's free, in most places in the USA and is accurate enough to get me by.

The rest of this section assumes you have a deal. If you don't have a deal then you can make one up. Pick a zipcode that you like and just use Zillow to look around. If you find a mobile home for sale, you can use that as your prospective deal for now as practice.

Open up www.Zillow.com.

Enter the zipcode of your prospective deal. You should see a bunch of dots on a map and a bar at the top with some filters. Enter the following into the filters:

1. The square feet (+- 20%)
2. Year (+-10 years)

3. A comparable make (You will probably have to click through all of the mobile homes and look in the salescopy for the make.)
4. As close as possible, preferably within the same park (if it's on its own land, find a mobile home on its own land as well).

One of the hardest lessons I had to learn as a real estate investor is that my property is only worth as much as someone is willing to pay for it. There are entire jobs built around comping houses (appraiser, real estate agent/broker, etc) and even these professionals won't agree on a price for any one house! Why? Because the value of your house is based on the values of all the other houses in the area. But none of those other houses might be exactly like your house so you need to fudge the numbers up or down in order to get something that is fairly reasonable. And you know what is really horrible? If someone in your area sold their house in a short sale, meaning they sold it quickly for much less than it was worth, then that home's sales price will go into your property's comp!

All that to say that these comp prices are all extremely relative and opinionated. The more comps you do, the more you'll have a general sense for what number feels right.

With stick built residential homes, it's easier to determine what people might pay because there are tons of houses and realtors make a lot of money selling them. Since there are a lot of them, more of them are more likely to be on the market. Since realtors make good money selling them, they're more likely to be on listing services (as opposed to FSBOs). The more that are on these listing services, the more data you have to compare the home you are trying to flip, wholesale, or rent.

Mobile homes are a little more difficult because there are fewer of them and the ones that are sold are more often sold FSBO because of the lower profit margins. Usually, homes that are sold FSBO do not appear anywhere online, so you cannot find what it sold for. It can also be hard to find exact information on it. What year it was built, how many square feet it has or what additions were made are more likely to be inaccurate or even just not included!

So, If you can't find any mobile homes for sale (or sold) that are exactly like yours, then increase your bounds incrementally until you can. For instance, change it to +- 15 years or increase the boundaries on your location. Again, these mobile homes should be selling or sold, preferably within the last 30 days, but up to 180 if you are desperate and in the same park.

Once you have a few mobile homes, look at their pictures to determine condition. You can do this for 2 conditions: the condition you're buying it in and the condition you are selling it in (if they are different).

So, how do you use these figures to determine the sales price?

- Step 1) Find 3-10 comparable mobile homes using the outline above
- Step 2) Divide the sales price with the square feet ($/square foot)
- Step 3) Multiply the $/sqft by the square feet of your prospective mobile home.

More on how to use them later.

Checking Your Work

You can also pay an online company to determine what your mobile home is worth for anywhere between $25 and $50. I would use https://www.nadaguides.com/Manufactured-Homes.

I would definitely leverage this tool to check out the value of your first ten prospective deals. Once you know that you're about as accurate as that site, then you probably don't need it anymore.

If you don't want to pay for someone to give you comps, then you can try to find other mobile home investors and ask them for help. I find that Facebook groups and REIA clubs are a great place to meet other investors who don't mind taking a second to look at your deal. Make sure you have completed Step 2 of due diligence before you start asking for someone to check your work!

When do I Hire an Appraiser?

Only hire an appraiser when you have your mobile home under contract. You can still negotiate with the seller after the home has been placed under contract. If you can show them there is hidden damage, they're usually ok with cutting the price. A good appraiser will find all of this damage and give it to you in an itemized report. This is perfect for both negotiation and having a contractor to do a repair estimate.

The Purchase Price

Flip

Flippers generally try to purchase a mobile home for 70% of ARV minus repairs. 70% seems to be the magic number that allows for profit even if you make mistakes. Even if you underestimate your repair cost or underestimate ARV, you should still turn a profit by following the 70% rule.

Let's look at some math to see how this works in reality. Let's use an example mobile home that has an ARV of $10,000 and a projected repair cost of $2000. What is your maximum purchase price?

$$(\$10{,}000) \times .7 = \$7{,}000 \ldots \text{ARV} \times .7 = \text{Adjusted ARV}$$
$$\$7{,}000 - \$2{,}000 = \$5{,}000 \ldots \text{Adjusted ARV} - \text{Repair cost} = \text{Maximum purchase price}$$

If you pay $5,000 to buy it and $2,000 to repair it, you are left with $3,000 in profit! Of course, there are a few more things you need to keep in mind but we'll discuss those later.

Rent

I take a different approach to rentals than other real estate investors. I want my mobile home rentals to be paid off within 2 years.

Why?

Mobile homes are cheap and they're all about cashflow. Since they're cheap, you can pay them off really fast. And the sooner they're paid off, the more cashflow you have.

I like to find how much I can rent these homes for, subtract the lot fee and capex, and multiply that by 24. (Because there are 24 months in 2 years). This roughly gives me the amount I need to pay off my mobile home in 2 years. Yes, there is some interest involved, but as long as it's less than 5%, it shouldn't be too much of an issue because we're paying this mobile home off so fast.

Let's say I'm going to make $1,400/month on a mobile home. My lot fee is $250 and I'm going to save 5% of the monthly rent for capex, so that's $65. That leaves me with $1085/month. That means I can pay a maximum of $23,640 for a mobile home in that park. That would get me an old double-wide or a pretty new single-wide!

Yes, some of that $1085 would go toward paying the mortgage. If I made a 10% down payment and took out a 10-year loan with a 5% interest rate, I'd have to pay about $500/month for mortgage, taxes, and insurance. The leftover $585 is where it gets interesting.

Depending on your debt tolerance, you can either save that up for another down payment (which you would have in a matter of 4 or 5 months) or you could throw it into your current mobile home's mortgage.

If you chose to put it in your current mortgage, you'd have it paid off in a little over 2 years, which is much better than waiting 30!

Personally, I don't mind debt, so I'd put it into a new down payment. As long as you aren't too overleveraged, it won't be an issue.

You might be wondering how I pay off this mobile home in two years if I take all of my extra money and put it into a down payment for another mobile home. The answer is that

I don't. I just use the two year maximum payment as an indication of if I have a good deal or not.

Usually, my loans are for a period of 20 years. Even if you are trying to pay your mobile home off within two years, I would suggest you also try for a 15+ year loan. After all, you can always pay your mortgage off early but you will have problems if you try to pay it off late!

Wholesale

Wholesalers need to understand the landlord and flipper's purchase price because they need to buy any mobile home for less than that. If you find a home that you think would be perfect for a renter, you know you're going to need to buy it for less than 70% of the ARV minus repairs because that is what the flipper will want it for.

For instance, if you find that same $10,000 mobile home, you're going to need to buy it for something less than $5,000 because you know that any flipper will want to buy it for $5,000 due to their formula. That means you're going to need to have a really good sense for estimating repairs because extra repairs will eat into your profit margin! Remember, wholesalers live off rock bottom deals. The only people who have these are extremely motivated sellers!

Another thing wholesalers need to keep in mind is the price of moving these units. If you find a mobile home that needs to be moved, it will cost anywhere from $5,000 to $10,000! Make sure you figure that into your calculations before you decide to sign a contract.

Sales Calculator

I have all the calculations you need to make a deal in my Mobile Home Deal Calculator at www.MateosMobiles.com/Mobiles.

How Much Can I Rent Them For?

Like selling a mobile home, the amount of rent you can charge also depends on the location and a whole host of other factors. For example, in the area where I live, I know investors who charge as much as $1,500 per month. To figure out how much you can charge, it's helpful to figure out why people even want to live in mobile homes in the first place.

Mobile homes are popular in areas where housing is expensive. In mobile home friendly markets, traditional real estate offers a bad deal for renters. For example, the average rent in San Francisco is $3,630 and the average apartment size is 750 square feet[12]. This is a ridiculous situation for most families.

Value for money is what mobile homes offer and that's how you ought to decide on the rental price of your property. In most areas, mobile homes are concentrated in mobile home parks. Parks bring their own idiosyncrasies to the table and you'll need to be aware of these.

Some parks don't allow homeowners to rent their homes out to tenants as I mentioned earlier. Make sure the park is okay with you renting out your property before you purchase or move a property there. There are additional rules to adhere to as well. Rules regarding noise, maintenance, and guests are important from the park's point of view. They typically hold the owner responsible, not the tenant. Some mobile home parks even place age limits on residents.

If your tenant breaks too many rules, you'll be faced with eviction. Usually, the parks give you some warning before they do this but in the worst case, eviction means you'll need to move your home out of the park and absorb the moving costs that come with it.

You can mitigate the risk of eviction by including the park's terms in your lease. If your tenant breaks enough rules that the park gets involved, you should immediately start the eviction process. Yes, it can get expensive but not as expensive as moving your entire home out of the park. This happens very rarely, especially if you do good due diligence when selecting your tenant.

Parks come with their pros and cons. The higher-end parks charge high lot fees. However, parks that charge such fees do so for a reason. They maintain a high standard of living within them and take care to ensure tenants are of a high quality.

The park will likely ask to screen your tenants before they can move in. These parks usually have more expensive lot fees but are very well maintained and boost your mobile home's value.

Lower lot fees are easier to manage but they can also mean that the park is of low quality. If the park is of lower quality, you can't charge as much to rent out your mobile home. Similarly, they will probably accept and expect lower standards of renters in these parks. This is a trade off because when the standards for renters fall, you run a higher risk of eviction.

It doesn't really matter which park you choose as long as you vet your tenants appropriately and the rental numbers work out. The best strategy I've seen is to try to rent out gently used double-wides. Families are more attracted to the space these homes give you, you pay pretty much the same lot fee and you can charge more for the space. Speaking of charging…

The Price of Rent

I also like to use free online tools to find my mobile home's approximate rent.

If there aren't any mobile homes for rent nearby, you can also look at what similar bed/bath stick-built houses are renting for in your area and discount that price by a few hundred dollars. For instance, in my area, a 3-bed, 2-bath rents for $2000 per month. So, I would try to rent out my 3-bed, 2-bath mobile home for $1500 per month.

If you want some professional help renting out your first few mobile homes, you can call around and find a mobile home friendly realtor. You will likely have to pay them a portion of the first month's rent, but it will be worth it in the end because they will tell you what the approximate rental rate for your mobile home is.

Some Case Studies

Name	Cash inflow	Cash outflow
Price of a gently used double wide mobile home		$30,000
Refurbishment cost		$1000

Lot rent paid in 1 year		$350*12 = $4200
Capex @5% of monthly rent		$50*12 = $600
Property Taxes @2.7% of property value per year		$810
Insurance		$1,000
Monthly rent earned in 1 year	$1000*12 = 12000	

You spent $30,000 purchasing the home and $1000 fixing up some minor issues. $30,000 is middle of the road for a used double-wide, so you didn't get a fantastic deal, but you did find a house that was pretty up-to-date and had good bones. This isn't the type of deal you'd look to wholesale as the seller likely wasn't very motivated (you probably paid just about what this mobile home was worth) but it's fine for someone who just wants to find a mobile home and rent it out.

We'll say in this example you paid cash for the home: $31,000.

Your yearly expenses (including upkeep and vacancy) are $6,610.

Your yearly rent is $12,000.

So that means you're going to "make" 12,000-6610=$5390 each year.

31,000/5390 = 5.7 years until you have recouped your costs. This is very fast, especially when you compare it to traditional homes, but it isn't fast enough for me. It's not a bad deal, it just doesn't meet my two year recoup rule.

What if you were patient enough to find a motivated seller who wanted to sell you their house for a bottom of the barrel price?

Name	Cash inflow	Cash outflow
Price of mobile home		$10,000
Refurbishment cost		$5,000
Lot rent paid in 1 year		$350*12 = $4200
Capex @5% of monthly rent		$50*12 = $600
Property Taxes @2.7% of property value per year (Just because you paid 10,000 doesn't mean that's what it's worth. I used $20,000 to calculate this)		$500
Insurance		$1,000
Monthly rent earned over five years @ $800 per month	$1000*12 = $12000	

How much does finding a motivated seller and fixing up the mobile home really net you? Let's assume it took you 3 months to fix up the mobile home, which means you paid 350*3 in lot fees while you were waiting to flip it.

Total spent acquiring the home: $16050.

Your expenses for 1 year are $6300.

Your rent collected for 1 year is $12000.
So, you would "profit" $5700 in 1 year.
You would have this mobile home "paid off" in 2.8 years. That's much better!

My Mobile Home Deal Calculator calculates all of this for you, so make sure you download it to analyze your deals!

How Can I Increase the Value of a Mobile Home?

Optics

You should never lie to your buyers, but you should do your best to make your mobile home look clean and pleasant. For instance, when you take pictures, you need to make sure they are clear, have good lighting, and highlight all of the positive factors of your mobile home. Similarly, when you write the description, you need it to sound exciting and appealing.

When prospective buyers actually come to look at the mobile home, you want to make sure that it has been given a deep clean and smells good. Open all the blinds and curtains to leverage the beauty of natural light. Prune the garden so that it looks nice and fresh. Etc.

Energy Efficiency

Adding energy efficient upgrades to your home is the easiest way to generate lots of long term value. Your tenants will also appreciate the lower utility bills.

Lighting is the first place to begin. Install energy efficient bulbs and appliances. These cost more but they last longer and will significantly reduce your running costs. Apply caulk and insulation to the outer frame to reduce the heat loss. You can also install energy-efficient windows, just make sure they adhere to the HUD code.

Place it on Your Property

Instead of looking to buy just a mobile home, consider financing the purchase of land and then moving a mobile home onto it. Not only will it decrease your lot rent but it will also help the home maintain value. My favorite way to invest in mobile homes is to buy my own land, subdivide it, and slowly build a park with gently used homes.

Paint

Painting the entire mobile home can cost you a couple thousand bucks but it will increase the curb appeal significantly. If you are flipping the home, new paint is an excellent way to breathe life back into it. If you're renting it, painting will help convince people that your mobile home is a nice clean environment to live in. (You only need to repaint every 5-10 years unless you have a particularly dirty tenant).

Always go with white for the interior. It's simple, blends in, and will be easy for your tenants to decorate.

Inexpensive Upgrades

Remember how I mentioned that you should install new bathroom fixtures and new cabinets in the kitchen? Well, these are examples of inexpensive upgrades that add a ton of value in the eyes of a prospective tenant or buyer. Replace old light fixtures with new ones and install new door handles. Remove dull looking ceiling lights with inexpensive pendants or chandeliers. All of these upgrades give your home a luxurious look and you'll be able to justify charging a higher rent.

Older mobile homes come with tired looking wooden kitchen cabinets. You can give them new life by painting them and fitting them with new handles. Consider upgrading the appliances in the home. Scratch and dent stores are a great place to find high-quality refurbished appliances and accessories.

Make it Immobile

I've been focusing extensively on manufactured homes thus far but a small subset of mobile homes actually have wheels on them. These aren't considered real estate and are actually listed with the DMV. To convert them to real property, remove their wheels and install a foundation for them to rest on. You'll instantly increase the value of the property.

Remodel Baths and Kitchens

Kitchens and baths are the two most important parts of any home. Remodeling them is also an easy way to instantly add value. Interior mobile home walls aren't load bearing so you can remove them to create additional space. If you find a kitchen that is partitioned, consider removing the wall so that there's more space for tenants to move around.

Similarly, consider installing better tubs and showers in the bathrooms. You'll probably be upgrading the piping of old homes, so why not go the extra mile and upgrade the fittings as well?

Floors

Mobile home floors are prone to gathering water that causes the wood to rot. Thankfully, floor panels are easy to replace. Subfloors might take more work but it's always a good idea to make sure they're top notch. A good floor is of no use if the subfloor is rotten. They're relatively inexpensive to fix and will increase the life of your home considerably. If you've replaced the subfloor, this is a good selling point since it assures the buyer that they're getting a home that is going to last for a while.

Reinstall Insulation

Insulation is a cheap component in the overall scheme of things but it can drastically increase or reduce your bills depending on how well it's been installed. Some estimates claim that a five percent reduction in insulation can lead to a drop of 54% in energy efficiency[2]. Check the roof cavity, the subfloor, and the walls for insulation.

THE INVISIBLE DEAL

If you're renting, remember that you don't need to remodel your mobile home with the most expensive material. You just need materials and fixtures that look nice. Sometimes, your handyman will have a source for paint, tile, and vinyl flooring that is cheaper than what you can buy as a regular customer. Make sure you ask them what their prices are before you buy it yourself!

6

STEP 4: PROFIT!

The previous 3 steps were mostly about figuring out if the mobile home you were looking at was worth buying. This chapter will show you how to buy AND sell your mobile home! Fair warning, you should only purchase a mobile home that looks like it is worth buying. Mobile homes are some of the least risky real estate to purchase because they are so cheap, but the old real estate adage still rings true: Turning down a bad investment is the best investment you can make!

Financing

If you choose to finance your purchase (which I recommend!), you have 3 options.

One choice is to try to get a conventional or personal loan from a bank or credit union. Make sure you are upfront about your intentions when you ask them if they will finance your real estate purchase. It's important to tell them that you will be buying a mobile home that may or may not come with land AND that it will be an investment property.

An equally good choice (depending on your credit) is to seek seller financing from the seller.

If neither of the above options work out, you can try to find a private lender who will lend you a chattel loan on good terms. There are many lenders who will lend a chattel loan, but you are much more likely to have a higher interest rate. If you do go with a chattel loan and the interest rate is above 5%, I recommend paying your mobile home off as fast as possible instead of saving for a down payment on another home. 5% is a very high amount and will seriously eat into your profit margins if you let it go to term!

Banks and Credit Unions

Many banks may see loaning you money as a risky proposition and turn you down, but some banks won't. As with most things in real estate, it's a numbers game. You might hear 100 people say "No" but all that matters is the one person who says "Yes".

If you go with a conventional loan, you should try to fill out as many online forms and visit as many banks as you can within a 14-day period. All of these banks need to do a hard inquiry on your credit score. One or two is fine but a lot of of hard inquiries will tank your score.

However, the companies that keep track of credit scores understand that most people want to shop around for a loan. So, to make that possible, all hard inquiries made within a 14-day period are counted as the same inquiry.

Following that logic, it's in your best interest to try to make two full weekends bank days (Some banks are closed or have reduced hours on Sunday, so plan for that). Any bank or credit union nearby will do, but I find that the smaller they are, the better.

Try to get pre-approved for any amount. If they won't pre-approve you for a conventional loan, you can either ask them if they'll approve you for a personal loan or if they will approve your business for a business line of credit.

Again, you are trying to get pre-approved right now (and only if you're a flipper or a renter) so you don't necessarily need to have an investment. Some banks may want you to have your potential investment ready. If you have to do it that way, so be it, but it will be a much more fast-paced experience.

Private Lenders

Another type of financing you can try to ask for is a chattel loan. Any property that isn't connected to the land it's on is considered chattel. There are many lenders who will finance these purchases. They're private lenders so the terms and interest rates they'll offer you will vary. However, the interest rates they give you will be higher than the FHA loans.

Seller Financing

If you can't get a loan from a bank, you can try to get one from the seller. This is called seller financing. Not every mobile home seller knows about this, so you might have to talk to them and see if they are interested. It is a common way to get a loan on a mobile home without having to go through a bank.

Owner- or seller-financing is attractive and common for mobile homes. In this scenario, the seller acts as a bank. The buyer approaches them and tells them that they'll pay a certain price for the home as-is but they'll pay a slightly higher price if they can make payments over five years (or any other term). The buyer pays the seller a down payment and receives the title in return. However, the seller places a lien on the property that is removed once all payments are made. Owner financing rates vary wildly based on how the seller wants to handle your deal.

Cash

As a bonus, I'll mention the 4th option - cash. New investors might make the mistake of thinking that Real Estate Investing is all about paying cash for properties. While some real estate investors do try to use only their own money, this is a very slow way to gain financial freedom.

Consider that you have $15,000. You decide to use it all to buy a mobile home with cash. Let's say this mobile home gives you profit of $700/month. That means that you will have $15,000 saved up again in one year and eight-ish months. That really isn't bad! And if you are debt averse, you might think that this is fine for you. You'd buy another one and then that would half the amount of time it would take for you to buy a 3rd, etc.

But what if you took out a loan instead and bought all three with $5,000 down payments? Let's say you take a loan for five years and now only make $400 per month per mobile home (because you now have a $300 monthly mortgage payment). You'd be making $1200 per month in profit!

You would generate another $5,000 down payment in 4 months and buy another mobile home on those same terms. Now you're making $1600 per month! All within one year.

That is the power of leverage. Real estate investing is powerful because people leverage their money to buy investments they couldn't normally afford. It's like magic if you do it right because you're pretty much making something out of nothing!

All that to say: You can use cash if you'd like, but it's far better to leverage your money and take out a loan. As long as you're making more than you spend each month, you're golden.

Buying a Mobile Home

Now that you've found a mobile home, have done your due diligence, and have financing in place, it's time to buy it! Schedule a time to meet with the seller. Introduce yourself, make a little small talk, and then get on with inspecting the mobile home.

Good quality homes typically won't fall into your lap. You'll have to work for them a little. This means getting to know the seller and building a relationship. Be more kind than you think you need to be. Make sure you always ask permission before you do anything to their property, like enter it, push on walls, go under the skirt, etc.

You can use the checklist I've listed at the link in the beginning of this book. This is an easily printable list that will help you look at the common problem zones with mobile homes and will help you establish its condition quickly.

Inspection

Take a good walk around the home and look at all of the points I highlighted in the previous chapters. Refer to your checklist and be rigorous with your process. It's better to overestimate damage than to underestimate it. Pay special attention to how you can upgrade the property cheaply and whether this potential exists. Once this is done, it's time to offer a price.

Offering a Price

When offering a price, it's best to limit your offer to two choices. If the home you're considering is old, you'll typically want to offer less than $10,000. Here's how you can frame your offer. Tell them that you noticed certain defects in their property and that it's going to cost you money to fix them. As a result, you can offer them $3,000 for the home.

However, if they fix the issue themselves, you can increase that offer to $7,000. Tell them you're ready to pay $3,000 right now for the home as is or $7,000 if they upgrade it.

This is an old negotiation tactic that can work for almost anything. When you give someone a choice, they are more likely to choose one than come back at you with a different offer. You can also use this choice method with seller financing. "I see you want $10,000 for this mobile home. I can either give you $6,000 today or pay a down payment of $2,000 now and paid you $8,000 with interest over the next few years."

Visiting the mobile home and estimating the repair costs is the last step of due diligence. Once you've plugged your repair estimate into the Mobile Home Deal Calculator, you will know exactly how much you are willing to pay. Remember, you are trying to craft win-win deals, so don't fall into the trap of overpaying.

Renting out or Selling the Mobile Home

Caveats on Finding Tenants

Bad tenants cause all kinds of issues. If you have to evict them, you'll have to pay a lawyer *and* the tenant might destroy your property. If your tenant causes problems in the park, the park manager will likely not let you renew your lot lease. Word might spread that you let bad tenants lease your mobile homes and ruin your reputation.

So, we need to do everything we can to find a good tenant. Luckily, there are three easy steps you can follow to **almost** guarantee you a great tenant.

1. credit check
2. background check
3. deposit

Credit checks and background checks can be done from online. All you have to do is search for a credit check and background check company on Google. You want to make sure that your tenants do not have any evictions previously and have at least a 680 credit score (or if the mobile home park credit score is higher, you want them to have that).

When you run a background check, make sure there isn't any criminal activity. You also want to make sure they haven't foreclosed in the past 7 years, and if they have, then you need to ask for a larger deposit.

As a landlord, it's never a good idea to let your tenant pay late. Enforce late payment fees religiously. Do not let your emotions get in the way of doing good business. If they fail to pay you for two months in a row or seriously break your lease agreement, start the eviction process.

Leases

I like to have www.RocketLawyer.com write up all of my legal paperwork. If you purchase a subscription with them, they will write as many legal documents as you could want, all for the price of $40/month. That's a pretty great deal!

You want to make sure your lease includes a lot of the same terms as the park. That way if the tenant breaks the park rules, they are also breaking the rules on their lease. You also want to make sure that you ask for first and last month's rent as a deposit and charge more if your tenant has animals. You can either charge per animal, or you can charge a flat fee for any animal. I normally do not care if they have waterless tank animals (such as snakes) but if they have a dog, cat, or fish, I'll charge an extra fee.

Why charge extra? Dogs and cats can destroy a property if they aren't properly trained, so the extra you collect each month might go towards replacing the carpet when they are gone. A fish tank can destroy the floor if brake. Trust me, 30 gallons of water on your floors is not an easy thing to rectify.

THE INVISIBLE DEAL

Advertising your Mobile Home for Rent

In most cases, you don't actually need a realtor to help you rent out your mobile home. You can do it on your own! It might take a little bit more work, but it's worth it in the end.

First things first, do you know what the number one factor to your listing is?

Pictures!

When potential renters are looking through listings, the first thing they will see is a picture. When they look at the picture, they will decide in a second if they want to look further. All you need to make your listing stand out are fantastic pictures. They are, by far, the most important part.

Thankfully, you can take stunning photos with your phone. Here are a few tips to get your started:

- Clean the room! Make sure there aren't any surfaces with water on it (they'll be shiny and distracting in photos) and that there is no dirt anywhere.
- Take pictures from the corner of the room from hip height.
- Always take photos in landscape format, not portrait
- Staging really helps renters see the potential of the home (you can hire a local staging company if you have the money).
- Keep your main light source behind you. If you don't, it makes the room look dark.

- Try to take photos when the sun is either rising or setting (the golden hour!) and open all the blinds or curtains to let in all the natural light. Natural light is usually better than artificial.
- Take people on a tour of your rental. You can start at the most beautiful room and go through the house as if you are giving them a tour. If you can include a Youtube video of an actual virtual tour, even better!
- Get your photos retouched by a seller on www.Fiverr.com. www.Fiverr.com is one of my favorite contractor websites. You can find someone who lives in a low cost of living country but does amazing work. They will beautifully edit your photos for about 5 bucks. If you don't want to pay for that, you can try your luck on www.pixlr.com, a free photo editing tool.
- Take a TON of pictures—that way you give yourself a lot of options later.

The first picture you put on your listing should be the most breathtaking one. Normally, that is the kitchen or the living room (especially if the living room is staged). After that, I like to put my photos in the order you would see them if you were touring the home.

Listing Description

After your beautiful photos drum up interest for your property, the potential renter will usually want to find out more! The next step is reading the listing. People today do not have a big attention span, so you need to make sure you put the most important part of your description in the first two sentences.

The words you use are important. They are what will really seal the deal with your renters. Since they likely know where this property is located, what the rental price is, and have a feel for how it looks inside, your advertising copy is the last step in setting you apart from others so that your potential renter gives you a call.

When you write these listings, write them in second person, meaning use the word "you". You want to frame the property and all of its rooms as a place where your potential renter will feel at home.

Part of this is knowing who you will be advertising to. Are you in an area with a good school and advertising to families? Are you near a tech hub, advertising to a young couple who work in tech? Are you in a college town, advertising to college students? Decide who your main audience is and brainstorm what these demographics would like in a rental property.

For instance, if you're advertising to families, then you should focus on how your property is great for hanging out as a family. Highlight some features that families would like such as a spacious kitchen or a built-in laundry room. If you are near any cool attractions, like a zoo, a great school, or even a park, then you should also mention those.

If you're advertising to a young couple, then you might want to highlight the nightlife nearby. Highways are also a major plus with this demographic because they have to commute to work. Also, I have noticed that most young couples have animals, so you will probably want to mention that you are pet friendly (if you are).

If you're advertising to college kids, make sure you mention how close your property is to campus or campus transportation. You also want to mention that it is a cozy place for studying and a great place to entertain. Make sure you specify that smoking is not allowed indoors but that you have a designated area outdoors where they can smoke.

You can either choose to be pet friendly or not with college kids. Some have pets but most don't. You can also choose to rent by the room to college kids. You can use the same process I described earlier about finding your purchase price to see what the going rate for a room is in that college town. Or, you can simply divide the monthly rent by the amount of rooms. Either way, make sure the utilities are in your name if you want to rent by the room because there will probably be turn over!

When you create your ad copy, you also want to create scarcity. "Hurry up and book your appointment before this beautiful bargain is taken!". Creating scarcity is a trick as old as advertising itself\. No one wants to miss out on a good deal!

If your park is exclusive or even if it is just well-maintained with great amenities, you want to be sure to highlight that. It makes people feel like they are going to live in a great, safe neighborhood that has a lot of neat activities.

Overall, keep your ads simple, short, and focused on the potential renters' wants and needs.

Examples

Your ad's sentence structure should be

First(ish) sentence: DESCRIPTIVE WORD - TYPE OF PLACE at/near - DESCRIPTION ABOUT LOCATION.
Second sentence: PRICE/month
Third sentence: Call NAME at NUMBER

Family Example

Affordable AND newly-updated 3 bed/2 bath with built in laundry room and all new stainless steel appliances in a very friendly community that just "feels like home". Wonderful schools and stunning views makes this neighborhood perfect for your family to both work hard and play hard. $1000/month. Call Mateo at 555 - 555 - 5555

Young Couple Example

Newly-renovated 2 bed/2 bath in a beautiful neighborhood that features walking trails, parks, and even a free community gym! If you rent here, you will be near I-35, I-45 and only 10 minutes from downtown. Pet Friendly! $1000/month. Call Mateo at 555 - 555 - 5555

College Student example

Very affordable room in a 2 bed/2 bath house located right by campus in a picturesque neighborhood! You will LOVE the open concept kitchen which is perfect for entertaining or studying! Smoking is allowed in designated areas. $500/room. Call Mateo at 555 - 555 - 5555

Where do I post these listings?

I like to post my ads on Facebook Marketplace, Craigslist and Zillow. Facebook Marketplace is by far my favorite because it is free, takes 2 minutes, and gives you really high quality inquiries. If you don't get a lot of interest in your post's first week, you can try reposting or "boosting" it. Boosting it will cost you some money but also gets your post out in front of more people. The more people who see it, the more likely you are to find one to rent it. That's why I like posting my listings on as many places as possible.

Craigslist is another place that gets your listing out in front of a lot of people. Unlike FaceBook, each post costs $5. It's not free but that's a really low expense to get your listing out in front of hundreds of potential renters. Make sure you open yourself up to calls, texts, and emails so that you cater to everyone's needs.

Last, but certainly not least, Zillow. When you post to Zillow, you post to a lot of different places - Zillow, Trulia, AOL real estate, HotPads, MyNewPlace, and MSN Real Estate. Zillow will cost you $10/month but they have a guarantee that you will get inquiries *or your money back*.

Post your listing to all of these apps. Some of them do cost money, but it's almost nothing. Especially when you compare it to the price of a vacancy.

I would recommend setting up an open house one Saturday from 11 to 3 so you can show your place to everyone all at one time. You could choose to show it by appointment, but I find it's much easier to manage if you just show it one time. If we are still suffering through a pandemic when you start investing, make a Youtube recording of your rental and send that.

Once you have someone who would like to apply to rent, screen them. If they pass, all you have to do is send them their lease! I like to use docusign for leases because it's digital, cheap, and easy!

Listing Your Mobile Home for Sale

You can sell your home through Facebook Marketplace, Craigslist, and Zillow in exactly the same way (just say it's for sale instead). If you really can't find someone to purchase your mobile home then you can try to sell with a realtor or on RedFin.

Wholesalers

If you're trying to wholesale, I would recommend Redfin over the MLS (with freelance realtors) because Redfin will take much less of your profit (1.5% instead of 6%). However, if you're wholesaling, it's best to try to and do it yourself for a few weeks. Post it on the free/cheap sites I mentioned and go to REIA meetings to see if anyone is interested in fixing up a mobile home.

Flippers

If you just completed a flip, then it will likely be easier to sell your mobile home. I would still recommend you try using the free/cheap sites I mentioned unless your mobile home comes on land. If it is attached to land, you can get a very high premium for it and can use a realtor. Most flippers like to outsource the actual sale of the property because they have other things to do. The margins are pretty high anyway, so the realtor fee fits fine in the budget.

Documents You'll Need

There are a number of documents associated with mobile homes that will prove ownership and other relevant information. Here they are in no particular order (EZ Mobile Home Buyer, 2018):

- Title - If the home isn't tied to the land then you'll have to get a title from the DMV. If it is tied to the land, you'll have a land title issued by the local county.
- Proof of Taxes - Save your prior property tax payment receipts to show to the buyer that you've paid all taxes. If you're buying a property you should ask for this as well.
- Bill of Sale - This document proves that the property has been sold from one person to another. Both parties will sign it and have it notarized.
- Certificate of Occupancy - This certificate is issued by the local government and it certifies that the building is in accordance with HUD codes and that it's fit for occupancy. Not every state requires this so you should check with the local offices.
- Fire Safety Inspection - Many states will require fire safety inspection of mobile parks and the properties located in them. You'll be given a fire safety inspection certificate so make sure you save it as proof.
- Home Inspection - This is the same as an appraisal and having proof of this will help you settle on a good price to base negotiations on.
- Park Rules - Parks have their own rules and regulations so ask the seller for a copy of these rules before

you buy a property. If you're selling, have the rules printed and handy for the buyer's convenience.

Types of Licenses

Every state has its own method of licensing people and professionals who operate in the mobile home space. Here are some of the licenses that you'll find (Fedro, n.d.):

- Manufacturer - This is a company that assembles mobile homes. They can be small or large
- Retailer - This is someone who offers mobile homes for sale to buyers. Depending on how many mobile homes you buy and sell in a 12 month period, your state might classify you as an active retailer.
- Broker - The middleman who facilitates the buying and selling of property.
- Mover - This is a person or entity who agrees to install and set up a mobile home. If you plan on moving homes you might need this license.
- Sales Agent - This person is an employee of the broker or retailer and receives compensation in exchange for completing a sale.

CONCLUSION

My hope for each of my books is always the same: give you an easy, step by step guide on a relatively unknown part of real estate investing. The world of investing is so much broader than what HGTV or even your REIA would have you believe. I hope that I've at least convinced you that mobile homes are a solid real estate investment worthy of further examination.

I'd love to hear one thing that you learned from my book in the review section. I am a new writer and I'm always ready to learn what I can do to make these books and guides better for you.

If there's one thing I want you to take away, it is that you need to take action. I gave you a lot of information but only you can decide what to do with it. Once I realized that reading hundreds of real estate books wasn't as important as hitting the streets and knocking on doors, my whole life changed.

It's really easy to get discouraged when you invest in real estate. There is a lot of rejection, hard moments and general stress… but it's all worth it when you cash that first check. If you need a safe space to vent, ask questions, or just hang around like minded individuals please check out my Facebook group at www.MateosMobiles.com/FB.

That said, I hope that this book gave you enough confidence to start investing today. The next step is very simple. **Take out your phone and set an alarm that goes off 30 minutes earlier than normal that says "LOOK FOR MOBILE HOMES"**. Do it. You won't regret it.

Let's rock this.

Mateo

REFERENCES

1. Kern A. (October 28, 2020). *Why Manufactured Housing Is the New Affordable Housing.* https://www.cpexecutive.com/post/why-manufactured-housing-is-the-new-affordable-housing/
2. EZ Homes. (2017, November 10). *Mobile Home Upgrades That Can Increase The Value Of Your Home.* (2017, November 10). https://www.mhomebuyers.com/mobile-home-upgrades/
3. EZ Mobile Home Buyer. (2018, December 28). *What Forms Are Needed to Sell a Mobile Home Quickly in 2019.* https://ezmobilehomebuyer.com/documents-sell-mobile-home/
4. Fedro, J. (n.d.). The Investor's Guide to Mobile Home Licenses. *BiggerPockets.* https://www.biggerpockets.com/blog/mobile-home-licenses
5. Ference, A. (2017, August 2). *How to Sell a Mobile Home: A Guide on Financing, Price, and More.* Real Estate News and Advice|realtor.com. https://www.realtor.com/advice/sell/how-to-sell-a-mobile-home/
6. Home Nation. (2020). *Different Types of Mobile Homes.* https://homenation.com/blog/guide-to-different-types-of-mobile-homes
7. Lange, J. (2013, September 23). *8 Ways to Buy Older Mobile Homes for Cheap.* CREOnline. https://www.creonline.com/8-ways-to-buy-older-mobile-homes-for-cheap/
8. Mueller, L. (2019, September 27). *How Much Does a New Mobile Home Cost?* Moving.Com. https://www.moving.com/tips/how-much-does-a-new-mobile-home-cost/

9. Obando, S. (2020, March 27). *Flipping Mobile Homes*. Millionacres. https://www.fool.com/millionacres/real-estate-investing/house-flipping/flipping-mobile-homes/#
10. O'Dell, C. (2020). *Should You Remodel An Older Mobile Home?* Mobile Home Friend. https://mobilehomefriend.com/should-you-remodel-an-older-mobile-home/
11. Phipps, M. (2020). *How Can I Increase the Value of My Mobile Home?* SF Gate. https://homeguides.sfgate.com/can-increase-value-mobile-home-55937.html
12. RENTCafé. (2020, February). *San Francisco, CA Rental Market Trends.* https://www.rentcafe.com/average-rent-market-trends/us/ca/san-francisco/

All images sourced from Pixabay.

Mount Laurel Library
100 Walt Whitman Avenue
Mount Laurel, NJ 08054-9539
856-234-7319
www.mountlaurellibrary.org

CPSIA information can be obtained
at www.ICGtesting.com
Printed in the USA
LVHW010233280821
696293LV00006B/1075